The story of the litt
Still dead. Still a

I AM NELSON
What happened next

Martina Mars

&
Addendum
Publishing

First published in Great Britain in 2022 by Addendum Publishing

A catalogue record for this book is available from the British Library.

ISBN 978-1-8383675-1-0

Cover design by BespokeBookCovers.com
All photos & images, including cover photos, author's own collection.

www.addendumpublishing.co.uk

For Auntie Marina
who one early Wednesday morning in February
after this book had been written
joined Nelson on the Other Side

And for Uncle Richard
who misses her an awful lot

CONTENTS

Chapter 1

THE STORY CONTINUES

Someone once told my mum that dogs are guardian angels in training. To which my mum replied, 'There's still a lot of training to be done then.'

That's because I wasn't exactly easy-going when I was still around. But she loved me anyway. LOADS! And so did my dad.

For those of you who don't know me: I am Nelson!

For you, I died a few years ago, but of course I am still very much alive – just not on your side of things. I've explained it all in the book my mum helped me write. It is called 'I AM NELSON' – of course! – and it's the true story of my life and death. And what happened afterwards. So, if you want to find out more, you can read all about me and my human family and friends in there.

And for those of you who already know all about me and remember me, I figured you would want to know what happened next.

And before you ask, yes, I'm still over here!

Now, if you've read my story, you are probably wondering how that could possibly be. Well… it's all to do with time.

When I told you my story before, my mum added a chapter at the end, called 'Wishful Thinking' to let you know that she believed with all her heart that I would come back. She was right, but that's not exactly *when* it happened. Let me explain.

You see, time flows differently over here. Between where you are and I am it kind of *stretches*. You know, like when you step on a piece of chewing gum that's stuck to the pavement; but because you've stepped on it, it now also sticks annoyingly to your foot, and then it stretches as you walk on. It's still the same chewing gum but now it's, at the same time, behind you on the pavement, and also with you, and in front of you, you know, stuck firmly to your foot.

It's the exact same thing with time.

It basically means a lot can happen on your side,

when only minutes have passed over here.

And that's how it's possible that what I am about to tell you happened *before* my mum finished writing the last chapter of my story. She didn't know this because I didn't tell her then. But I'm telling her all about it now, so she can pass it on to you.

People say 'Every ending is also a new beginning'. Doesn't make the ending any less painful. And doesn't necessarily make the new beginning bright either. But it *is* new. And since you don't have a choice in the matter anyway, you might as well get on with it and make the best of things.

And that's what my parents did after I died. As best they could.

At times it was really hard and my mum kept saying to my dad that sometimes life seems to be all about saying goodbye. And that every new hello only leads to another goodbye. People around my parents tried comforting them by saying stuff like 'When your time is up, it's up. That's just the way it is.' What they really mean to say is that there's nothing you can do about someone dying, so you better accept that that's a fact of life and just move on. My mum would tell you that that's an easy thing to say and a much harder thing to accept. And harder still is to let go. Because you just never know what is letting go and what is giving up hope.

My mum once read somewhere that loss is the price of love. But unfortunately that means the more you love someone the more it hurts to lose them. And if you love someone an awful lot, it will hurt an awful lot, too, when they're gone. That's what happened with my parents and me.

The funny thing about death is that it isn't so bad after all. Not for the person who's doing the dying anyhow. But it's very hard for the ones who are left behind, because we are not really allowed to tell you that we're still around. There are ways around it, but even when we somehow manage to give you a sign, half of the time you don't believe that that's what it is. Extremely frustrating!!

But like I said, dying isn't so bad after all. It's only eerie for you because you don't know what over here is like. And I'm not allowed to tell you.

I mean, sure, when I first got here it freaked me out a bit. But then you get used to it. And at first you think 'Great, now I can go anywhere I like and nobody can tell me to stay at home alone anymore!' and you can spend every single second with the people you love. Even in places where they don't allow dogs to enter.

But then you realise that you're not *really* there for them because they can't see you, and that you can't do the things you used to do anymore. Not like before anyhow, because you don't have the same body anymore.

And so not even my Rule Number One, 'DON'T TOUCH MY BOTTOM! OR MY BACK!' applies any longer because people can't touch me now. Not really anyhow. On the one hand, kind of handy. Then again, not half as entertaining.

And no matter how hard you try, you just can't make the people you love see you, and it *really* isn't nice to be ignored. Oh, and let me tell you, it's more than a little boring! And at the same time there is so much to see and do over here. So you end up checking up on your family less and less, until you finally leave for good.

Someone over here explained to me once that the whole thing is a bit like when people move house. At first everything is new and exciting, and you explore everything that's new, and you're having fun. But then you start feeling a bit homesick for the place where you used to live before. And so you go back for a visit. Only now it's not quite the same because you don't live there anymore and it hurts a bit to remember how things used to be.

So you leave again and get on with your new life, and in the end you only go back occasionally, and over time even less and less so, because there really isn't anything there for you anymore, apart from your memories.

And eventually it's easier and less painful to leave it all behind.

Same with being dead.

At first you have great fun checking out all there is to check out over here, but at the same time you miss your family an awful lot, and so you keep rushing back to them all the time, because all you really want is to be with them, never mind that they can't see you any longer. Often right in the middle of doing something, too, because all it takes over here to go places is a thought and *whoosh* you're where you want to be. Bit startling to say the least but eventually you get used to it. Kind of.

But after a while the whole thing gets a bit stale and more than a bit painful because you realise that for some strange reason even though people can't see you, somehow they can feel you, and it always makes them sad. And you can't lick their faces to make them feel better. So you both end up being sad and frustrated.

And that's when you know it is time to move on.

Or in my case, try to find my way back home for good.

I've tried coming back to your side of things quite a few times already, but it didn't work out the way I had planned it to. Ask my mum, she dreamt about it. Then again, she isn't sure that what she dreamt is true, so no point asking her after all.

You see, the problem with coming back for good is that you end up in a new body and that you forget all about your old life. The one you lived before. So that you're free to learn new things and stuff, they tell me. And then you only remember what you forgot when you're back over here once more. Highly annoying! I won't give up though, just wait and see!

When I first arrived over here and began to explore the place, I suddenly remembered all the stories my parents had been telling people about the life they had lived before I came along. Especially all the things about my furry siblings (dogs – yes, *and* cats!) who had lived with them and died long before my mum and dad found and adopted me. But since I only knew bits and pieces and I *was* **rather curious about all the other furry members of my family**, I decided to find out all the rest and what I didn't yet know.

You see, that's the great thing about being over here. You can go anywhere you want to and find out all you ever wanted to know about anyone or anything.

What I knew already was that there were five of us in total.

First there was DeNiro, then Nefertiti, then Alfred, then Oscar, and finally, and most importantly of course, ME! But I was the only one my parents actively looked for *on the line* and adopted. The others all came to them one way or another by themselves. Kind of. I'll tell you how in a moment.

Oh, and by the way, when I say there were five of us, that's obviously not counting all the many other animals that crossed my parents' path but didn't get to stay.

Like the baby seagull my parents found outside our house one evening. The one with the broken wing. When my mum and dad found her lying on the street they really didn't know what to do, so they called the wild animal rescue people for help. But unfortunately they were WAY too busy to collect one little baby seagull that day because it was spring, and lots of baby seagulls get hurt during spring when they try to fly for the first time. Or fall out of their nests. Or when they get their wings caught in some wire or on some spiky bits people put on their roofs to ward them off. Never understood why some people do that and why they hate having seagulls around so much. After all the seagulls were living by the sea long before those people came along. It's their home!

Anyway, because the rescue people couldn't come immediately to save the injured baby seagull that evening, they told my mum and dad to cover her with a towel, put her in a cardboard box and keep her safely in our garden until such time when they were less busy and could pick her up.

Problem was, we don't have a garden.

But my parents couldn't just leave the struggling little seagull lying on the street in front of our house. And not just because there are bad people about who will often kill or maim injured animals when they're down and can't defend themselves, as the rescue people pointed out.

And yes, they really do, and that's the horrible truth.

Anyway, by now it was getting late, and so my dad went inside to fetch one of my towels to cover the little seagull with. I'm not quite sure what she made of my smell – and my hair – on the towel, but then again, I'm not even sure if seagulls can smell in the first place. I reckon not, or else they wouldn't eat all the yucky, stinky stuff I have seen them gobble up over the years.

Unfortunately, my mum and dad didn't have a cardboard box either to put the baby seagull in, so she ended up in our laundry basket instead. With lots of soft towels all around her for cushions. And then she got to sleep in my dad's studio, among the books and the sheet music. Right next to our bedroom, so my mum could check up on her all night long. And before you ask, yes, during her entire stay I was on my best behaviour. Didn't bark at her once. Didn't even sniff her. Mainly because my parents had closed the bedroom door so I couldn't.

I'm not quite sure what the seagull made of the whole change of scenery – probably never had been inside a house before. And she most certainly never had had a sleepover with two humans and a dog before.

And come the next morning she also got to drive in our car, because that's how my mum ferried her over to the rescue people's place so they could finally help her and hopefully fix her broken wing.

I reckon deep down the little seagull *was* grateful someone had helped and saved her, but I bet she was also mightily glad to see the back of us all.

In the weeks that followed I waited to see if she would fly by and visit us, seeing that she was now almost part of the family, but she never did.

We never saw her again, but I'm sure she had quite a few stories to tell when she finally got home to her own parents again.

And I bet nobody believed her!

But enough of that already. Here's what happened next.

Chapter 2

WHAT HAPPENED NEXT

My mum says the first year after someone dies is always the worst. She calls it the horrible *Year of Firsts*, because you are doing every single thing for the first time without the person you have lost. In my parents' case, the first night without giving me my goodnight doggie biscuit and then covering me with my favourite blanket, the first breakfast without feeding me first, the first lunch and no one there to beg for a share of it, the first dinner (ditto), the first walk through the Country Park or along the beach without me running around like mad, and endless sticks and pebbles on the ground and no one there to pick them up anymore. The first holiday without having to pack all my things, the first birthday (for either one of us), the first

Christmas without anyone trying to nip Heloir, the little toy deer, in the butt, the first... I could go on for hours!

And the *Year of Firsts* doesn't wait until you're ready for it either. Oh no, it has a life of its own and it starts the very second you lose someone you love.

My mum says it's just an endless list of painful firsts until you've done all the things you used to do together for the first time without the one you love.

And even then some things don't lose their sting, especially if you used to do them together loads. My mum still looks in the back mirror every time she drives our car, remembering how she used to catch a glimpse of me in the back, and my dad still can't walk past a stick that's lying on the ground without thinking of me. Sometimes he still picks it up and throws it for me, even though I'm not there any longer, and then he wonders if I am chasing it over here on the Other Side.

And for the longest time my parents would continue taking bits of food from their plates and holding them just above where my begging nose used to be. And then they would look at each other with that look in their eyes that tells me that they still miss me very much.

And sometimes there are firsts even after the *Year of Firsts* has passed, and those are the ones that hurt the most. Because you didn't expect them.

And then there are the bad memories. And the very sad ones. But my mum says you have to look them firmly in the eye and face them, too. Because if you don't, they start eating you up from the inside. And if that means that you'll have to cry, and cry, and cry some more, then that's what you'll have to do to get through it. At least that's what my mum did when I died. Never saw so much liquid coming out of anyone's eyes!

And then she started to write everything down so she would never forget me. Not that there was ever the slightest chance that she would have. She has all those memories firmly lodged in her heart.

At the end of the horrible *Year of Firsts*, my parents marked the anniversary of the day I had died by lighting a candle and hugging each other tightly, and by having a final good cry about it all.

And then there were no more firsts, only an endless list of things and dates to remember the good and the bad times by.

It was also roughly around the time when my parents didn't feel me around so much anymore. I could have told them that that was down to the fact that I was coming back less and less. Mainly because it hurts to remember, but also because I was doing a lot of exploring and… um… *other* stuff… Can't tell you more. Like I once said, it's not allowed and the pages just go blank when I do.

My Auntie Barbara was one of the first people to comment on it. After the incident of my pushing hard against her leg, because she had dared to empty the bin without my permission during my parent's first holiday without me, Auntie Barbara was slightly reluctant to enter our house again on her own.

During my parent's next trip, the one to North and South America I already once told you about, I went with them, so Auntie Barbara didn't run into me while she was house sitting, which calmed her nerves enormously. She didn't know I wasn't around, so she ended up talking to an empty house instead of me. Just in case. You know, along the lines of 'Hello Nelson, I'm just going to have a look around. I won't bother you, and I most certainly won't touch anything that's been left on the floor, so no need to attack my leg again…' – which of course I would have if she had.

And then a few months later, my mum and dad went to a Spanish island for a breather. It coincided with the anniversary of the day when I had had my amputation the year before, and my mum got it into her head that she had to carry me around the whole day (as a ghost) just in case I was still there and needed comforting. And so she did. The entire day, until her arms were cramping, even though she couldn't be sure I was really there. But I was, and it was awfully nice to be carried around in her arms once more. Even though I don't have a body like before anymore and had to pretend that I still do.

But when my parents got home from that trip, my mum told my dad that she wasn't so sure anymore that I was still around. And Auntie Barbara told her that she also didn't think that I was hanging around any longer. Not in her house and not in ours. I reckon a part of her was still mightily relieved that I hadn't attacked her leg again.

They're not completely correct of course, but I *was* kind of busy doing other stuff at the time.

Also, I had finally figured out that, more often than not, it makes people cry when you pop over to visit them. Not sure why that is, but it happens almost every time one of us comes to visit one of you. Like I said before, even when you don't see us, somehow you can feel us and it makes you sad.

And since I love it when my parents are happy and laugh, and I hate to see them cry, I decided to stay away.

Also, I was starting to feel ever so slightly bored with the routine and wanted to explore more things over here.

A little while earlier, just slightly before the horrible *Year of Firsts* finally came to an end, something else had started to happen that was completely out of the ordinary. All of a sudden people started to die. In droves! And no, not like cattle – nobody had raised them to eat them. I just mean WAY more than usual. All around the world. We literally had new arrivals over here every single second. And I mean LOADS of them.

I didn't really understand why, but I heard people on your side blaming it on someone called *Pan Demic*. No idea who that is. The only 'Pan' I ever knew of was a jolly old fellow who got terribly irate when people confused him with the devil every time they happened to catch a glimpse of him in the woods where he lived. Just because he has horns. And hooves. But he wouldn't have harmed a fly, and definitely not people or other animals, so I reckon he wasn't the *Pan Demic* who was causing so much mayhem your side of things.

At the same time all those people were turning up over here, people your side of things stopped going outside. It was the weirdest thing. But all the wild animals *looooved* it. They could pretty much do whatever they liked on the streets, whenever they fancied to. For them it was almost back to the good old days before humans made their lives a misery.

Also, the air wasn't so stinky anymore because people weren't using their cars so much. But I guess, it wouldn't have been so much fun for me had I still been around, because I couldn't have gone for all my walks with my parents all of the time like we used to.

Another sad thing that happened was that people stopped giving each other *mimos*, you know, cuddles, and kisses. I would have hated that if I had still been around.

And then all of a sudden people began to wear muzzles. I couldn't believe what I was seeing! I used to HATE muzzles when I was still alive, and I can't think of a single reason why anyone would put one on of their own free will! And as if that wasn't bad enough, the muzzles people started to wear didn't even have holes in them for breathing. Beats me why! I could barely breathe with the one the vet forced me to wear whenever I had the misfortune of having to visit him. And *that* muzzle had plenty of holes in it.

But even my parents started to wear them. My mum even bought some colourful fabric and sewed herself one??!!!

I only learned some time later that people didn't wear their muzzles because they were being naughty or so they couldn't bite anyone else, but to avoid getting ill. Bit weird, if you ask me, never made me less ill when I was forced to wear one. Only made me more furious and irate.

But when people first started wearing their muzzles, I thought that maybe they did it because they finally wanted to find out how it felt having to wear one. You know, because they always make us dogs wear them at the vet's. And then I figured that maybe trying out what that felt like made people feel REALLY sorry for us, and that was the reason why they started adopting more and more dogs during the time *Pan Demic* forced them to stay at home.

In fact, people got so much into the whole adopting-a-dog thing, that when all the rescue centres had been emptied, and all the puppies around had been bought, some nasty people even took to stealing other people's dogs to sell them. Which made my mum wish that I was still around because she said she would have *loooved* to see the thief's face when they tried it on with me. She says they would have had me dangling off their thieving hands in two seconds flat and would have borne the scars of the encounter for the rest of their life.

Ahhhh yes, it would have been nice!

As it was, my parents were forced to stay inside for long periods of time, because *Pan Demic* apparently didn't want people to work anymore. Not outside their homes anyhow. So my dad just got on with composing, and since there weren't any acting jobs to be had anymore, my mum got on with writing down what I was telling her.

I also spent quite some time hanging out in all the places my parents and I had visited on our holidays together, because I was hoping they would come and visit me there. But they weren't allowed to. And by the time people were allowed to travel again, my parents didn't have the time to do so anymore, because they were too busy working. Thanks a lot, *Pan Demic*!

Not long after my mum had finally finished helping me write my story, she began to wonder if I really would be able to find my way back home for good again. Since she also wasn't exactly sure when that might be, she began to look for me everywhere. Not frantically like I would for a bone, but just now and then, mostly *on the line.* And mainly she just kept an eye out, just in case.

It became a bit of a joke between my parents,

because they weren't sure what they would do if I was reborn as, say, a horse and suddenly turn up on their doorstep. Because, you see, my mum firmly believes she would recognise me, never mind which new shape I'd be in. And I reckon she is right.

She saw many dogs over the many months that followed, but not one of them looked like they could be me. Only once did she become excited, when she came across the picture of a little rescue dog that had been born a few months after my death. Somebody with an even weirder taste for names than my mum had called the poor thing 'Butter', can you believe it?!!

My mum swore there was something in his eyes that reminded her of me, but neither she nor my dad were completely sure. And since Butter was in a rescue centre in Bahrain, and thanks to *Pan Demic* nobody was allowed to travel anyway, they couldn't just hop over to visit him to find out once and for all if he was or wasn't me.

But it niggled at my mum enough that she kept coming back to look at his photo time and time again.

In the end my parents decided to ask the rescue centre for a video of young Butter in motion to help them make up their minds. But unfortunately they never got a reply, even though my mum contacted them a few times about it. And then one day, when my mum looked at Butter's details *on the line* again, she saw a notice next to his photo stating that Butter had been adopted.

It really made my mum cry, but then my dad told her that he didn't think it had been me and anyway, even if it had been, they had tried, and then it maybe wasn't meant to be that we were reunited.

Don't look at me, I'm not allowed to tell you either way.

Anyway, after that my mum stopped looking for me *on the line*. At least that's what she told people. Of course, you and I both know that's a lie. She will never stop looking. And neither will my dad.

Chapter 3

BILLY

Do you remember that my mum sometimes used to say that on the outside I was a mixture between Jack Russell and Corgi, but on the inside I could be a right little Shih Tzu at times? Well, to me that was really two insults neatly wrapped into one. The first one is obvious – you would have known *exactly* what she meant by the way she said it. But it was also an insult because I REALLY didn't like Shih Tzus. And Lhasa Apsos. And Cocker Spaniels. And Springer Spaniels. Make that ANY type of Spaniel. And...

But I digress.

Now, given my intense dislike for Shi Tzus, it was rather ironic what happened roughly a year or so after I had died.

During the time when all the people were dying and *Pan Demic* forced everyone else to stay inside their homes, my mum, in her wish to help and do something useful since all acting and artistic work had come to a full stop, decided to volunteer for a well-known charity that helps elderly and infirm people to look after their animals when they cannot do it themselves anymore. You know, like finding someone to walk them and to foster them when their human parents need to go to hospital or feel unwell. Stuff like that.

So my mum signed up as a volunteer with that charity, and then she waited to hear if anyone needed her help. But when the people at the charity finally found a dog in our area that urgently needed someone to walk him, guess what breed he turned out to be. Oh yes, a little Shih Tzu! What a lovely little curve ball that was! I couldn't believe my eyes!

Luckily for him, by then I had already been over here for some time and had... um... mellowed a bit. Not much, but just enough to not have a go and try to freak him out by ghosting around every time he happened to lounge around on MY sofa.

He got lucky that things are different now. It's really weird, but once you're over here, you sort of *feel* differently and you somehow *know* more. And of course you learn new things every day.

So stuff that bothered me a lot when I was still alive doesn't matter so much to me now. I can even look at a postman now without wanting to rip his pants to shreds. Well, ok, *almost*. The thought is still there at the back of my mind, but it's somehow less... urgent.

And luckily for the little Shih Tzu my mum got to walk, I'm less jealous than I used to be. *Marginally...*

Anyway, his name is Billy, and he is very different from me in every single way. He is very calm and laid-back, and he lets anyone who wants to touch him, touch him at any time they want to and for any length of time they want to... You're getting my drift!

He will also NEVER, EVER growl and flash his teeth at anyone (not that he could even if he wanted to – because of his underbite) and – can you believe it – in all the years of his existence he never once laid down any rules of his own!

He doesn't like sticks, completely ignores pebbles, is always friendly with everyone he meets, be that children or grown-up people, other dogs – even cats and birds! – and on the whole is as threatening as a soft, fluffy pillow.

The only thing he and I have in common is the fact that he likes his walks and that my mum washes his paws (and bottom) afterwards. He isn't too keen on the whole washing business either, but unlike me he just stands there and lets her get on with it.

But he doesn't like to be blow-dried afterwards, and he doesn't care much for what my mum calls *'Bürsten, bürsten!'* either, you know, to be brushed for hours on end, whereas I used to *LOOOOVE* it! Simply couldn't get enough of it. In fact, got so obsessed with it that I once half ate the brush when my dad stopped using it for the day. It's still in the drawer of the coffee table in the living room, bite marks, bits of my hair and all. Go check if you don't believe me.

Nope, Billy never once reminded my parents of me, which made things so much easier for them because they say it took the guilt away. You know, for looking after another dog, albeit on behalf of someone else.

You see, that's partly why my parents don't want to adopt someone else, because they are afraid I might feel they had replaced me. They just don't realise that there is no danger whatsoever of that ever happening – I'm unique! Also, some other dog who's been abandoned to their fate could probably do with all the love my parents have to give and that otherwise would kind of go to waste. And I know they will never forget me. How could they?!!!

So anyway, when my mum started walking Billy because his own mum was too ill to do it herself, at first I started to tag along every single time. But after a while it wasn't really interesting enough for me to do it all the time. I mean, I know all the walks, after all I have been there and done them a million times myself, and also, right now I quite frankly have better things to do.

But occasionally I still go with them, if only to dictate the next bits of my story to my mum. I love it when she stops to listen and sits down under a tree along the way to write down what I tell her. Invariably she doesn't have a pen and paper with her when that happens, and then she has to frantically type it all down on her phone and somehow send it to herself *on the line*. And then she smiles, and sometimes she even laughs out loud, and that makes me very happy.

And Billy... well, Billy waits patiently all the while for his walk to resume.

And before you ask, no I don't use him to hitch any rides. You know, as in quickly joining with him to say hello to my parents.

Well, ok, so it *did* happen, but only once, and then completely by accident. I swear!

The night it happened, Billy was snoozing on my sofa next to my mum – not up on top where I always used to sleep – and I happened to be around, checking up on what was going on back home. Only, at that precise moment I heard my dad come home in our car and I got really excited because he always used to pick me up to park the car with him and then walk back home with me.

So next thing I knew, I was somehow inside Billy, jumping up at the window to make sure it was really my dad who was coming home, and then racing down the stairs, barking 'I'm coming, Papá! Wait for me!' as loud as I could.

It only lasted a few seconds, and then I snapped out of it and found myself back over here once more. And Billy was left standing rather dazed and bewildered by the front door wondering how on earth he had gotten there.

But of course my mum guessed immediately

what had happened, because Billy NEVER behaves like that when my dad comes home. Don't get me wrong, he likes my dad, but he very much prefers to hang out with my mum, because she's the link to his own mum. In fact he never lets her out of his sight, because she's the one that picks him up from his own home, and more importantly, brings him back again. And although Billy gets on really well with my dad, he's really not that bothered whether my dad comes or goes. And he most certainly NEVER barks with joy when he sees him.

So my mum realised that very moment that it had been me inside Billy, hitching a ride, and she got really excited and kept asking Billy 'Is that you, Nellie?'. But of course by that time I was already long gone, and so Billy just gazed up at her fondly, wagging his tail, as he always does.

Oh, and he totally ignored my dad.

When my mum first started to walk Billy, she did it twice a week for two hours at a time. But then, a few months into the experience, Billy's mum needed an operation and so Billy got to stay with my parents for a few weeks while his own mum was getting better. He didn't complain, but I'm sure he was wondering what on earth was going on.

Also, it was a very hot summer that year, and Billy has a lot of fur. It doesn't come out by the bucket load like mine used to do – in fact it doesn't come out at all. It just sticks to him, whereas mine just stuck to everything and everyone else. But all that curly fur means that Billy gets very hot in summer. Which is why my mum covered him in a wet blanket to cool him down, especially when they were going somewhere in the car. And Auntie Dee said he looked like an *Ewok* with a hoodie.

It was also during that time my parents first noticed that Billy never lets my mum out of his sight because he is mega worried that she will leave the house without him. And then how would he get back home to his own mum? Unfortunately that means he will literally get up from wherever he is currently resting, every single time my mum gets up to go somewhere else in our house. And let me tell you, my mum moves around A LOT. Up the stairs, down the stairs, from one room to the next and back again. And poor Billy always right behind her, never mind how tired he is.

My mum observing this felt at once very sorry

for him. So the next time they were both relaxing on the sofa together and my mum had stuff to do in another room, she turned around to Billy and explained to him slowly and exhaustively, that she was going to get up in a moment, but not to worry because that didn't mean that she was going to leave the house, that in fact she was only going down to the kitchen for a moment to make herself a cup of tea (and possibly a bite to eat), and that it was therefore completely safe for him to remain on the sofa and await her return.

What a complete waste of time that was!

Because no sooner had my mum finished with all the talking and the explaining and got up to leave the living room, one tired little Shi Tzu got up immediately too and followed hot on her heels.

So then my mum tried to simplify matters and told Billy to 'Stay!', which he did, but only for a few seconds, and as soon as she was out of sight and he couldn't hear her voice anymore either, he raced after her in utter panic.

Over the next few days my mum mulled the whole thing over, and in the end she came up with this little singsong around the word 'stay' which she uses to this day.

Basically, whenever she needs to leave the room now she will sing 'Stay, stay, stay...' on a never-ending loop until she comes back to wherever Billy is. No matter how long it takes or where in the house she goes, or what she does. Yep, even when she goes to the toilet. That way Billy always knows where she is and can let her walk about without worrying she might leave without him.

It really works too, although it *does* get a bit tiresome for my dad. Especially when my mum takes ages to get back to Billy and my dad is busy composing. But he puts up with it because he feels sorry for Billy, too.

A few months earlier, during the time when people still weren't allowed to go outside for more than an hour each day because of *Pan Demic*, everyone had been busy watching the animals outside their windows take over the world once more. In some places goats were venturing into towns, foxes felt safe enough to lounge around all day in public places, and the birds especially were shouting from the roof tops how happy they were that the air was clean for once and that they could go about their business undisturbed. My dad was so inspired that when he got his next commission, he composed a piece about them for flute and piano, called 'The Birds'.

A few months later, when *Pan Demic* at last allowed people to meet up again in small groups, my dad's piece was finally premiered during a private performance, in front of only a handful of people, including the lady who had commissioned it.

But of course, Billy at the time still happened to be with my parents on account of his mum only slowly getting better after her operation. So my parents decided to take him with them to the performance. This was a bit of a risk because at the time they didn't know him that well. And also they weren't sure what his taste in music was like. If you remember, there was many a piece that would set myself off and make me howl at the top of my lungs when I was still around.

But seeing that Billy seemed very placid and didn't display any of my own unique character traits, and also because my parents didn't really have much of a choice as they didn't want to leave him home alone, they decided to let him come along.

I could have told them that that was a rather foolish idea…

At first everything went according to plan. The few invited people arrived, and everyone made sure they wore their muzzles and sat as far away from each other as possible. The pianist and the flautist took their place on the stage, and Billy made himself comfortable on the bench right next to my mum and her friend. My dad held a short speech and then sat down himself. Silence descended and everyone settled down to enjoy the performance.

Unfortunately… that was the precise moment Billy chose to pass wind. At length, and of the silent but deadly variety. And not even the muzzles everyone was wearing could filter out the stench.

But at least hers hid my mum's blushes because she realised that nobody could be completely sure who the culprit had been and she didn't want to be accused of anything. Her friend was reduced to staring at her wide-eyed and nostrils flaring behind her muzzle because the smell was just so bad.

Luckily the people in the front row hadn't noticed, nor had the musicians, and so the performance began.

Unfortunately that's also when it became apparent that Billy was very much getting ready to sing along, because he was starting to make wobbly sounds at the back of his throat as soon as the flute started to play. All my poor mum could think to do in her panic was to clamp both her hands firmly over Billy's ears, her reasoning for this being that if Billy couldn't hear the music, he also wouldn't be able to sing along.

Luckily for her, Billy has hanging ears, not pointy, upright ones like me. So she grabbed them both like two furry face cloths and unceremoniously pulled them right over his eardrums, all the way down towards his chin, thus making it impossible for him to hear a thing. And then she hung on tight until the end of the performance while Billy did his very best to try to shake her off.

My mum says it was the longest 5 minutes and 15 seconds of her life. But she won the battle. Billy, not being able to hear a thing, and also being thoroughly confused by my mum's apparent clinging obsession with his ears simply shut up.

He got a treat at the end of the performance and was none the wiser. The same went for the audience. But my mum sweated so much she needed a shower afterwards.

After that my parents didn't take Billy to performances anymore. But he still got to hang out with them twice a week, and after a while not only for two hours but for the whole day each time, and he still does to this very day. Occasionally he gets to stay for a sleepover, too, but contrary to me, he doesn't mind that my parents wriggle about an awful lot when they sleep – like I said, Billy is WAY more placid than I ever was, and he doesn't mind a lot of things I would have strongly objected to.

35

Whenever Billy comes over to stay, my mum picks him up, takes him for walks and at the end of the day brings him back to his own home again, which means that he also gets to travel in Raúl, our car. What? You didn't think just because it's only a car it doesn't have a name? You really should know my mum better by now!

Anyway, when Billy gets to travel in Raúl, he sits right next to whoever is driving, in the front. Usually on someone's lap. Not in the back. The back is mine. And it's also still completely covered in my white hair. Not even the people at the car wash who tried to valet it one time got my hair out. My dad says it's tenacious, just like me.

Talking about car wash, the other day my mum took Billy along with her when Raúl needed to be washed because the seagulls had pooped all over him. Again!

And – can you believe it – Billy just sat there placidly and calmly watched the brushes come and go and wash the car all over. I couldn't believe my eyes!

And my mum who was observing him do ABSOLUTELY NOTHING, was grinning from ear to ear during the entire time because of course she remembered that I would almost smash the car windows with my teeth each time *we* went to the car wash, in my frenzied effort to get at the insolent brushes, to teach them a lesson for daring to touch our car.

Makes me still cross just thinking about it, even though it's been a while…

Billy also got to stay over at my house at Christmas, so his own mum could go and visit with her family who happen to have a bigger dog that doesn't like him and once had a go at him.

Billy met Heloir on that occasion, you know, the little white toy deer my brother Alfred had so objected to. The one I myself had nipped on the sly a few times myself. But Billy wasn't really interested. He completely ignored Heloir. But he did enjoy hanging out with my parents and getting lots of treats over the holidays in the process.

And then he was very happy to go back home to his own mum again. Because he loves her an awful lot, just the way I love my parents.

Chapter 4

OF MICE

During the first winter after my death, mice moved into our attic for the first time ever. Probably because they figured that since I wasn't around any longer, they might as well take advantage of the situation.

As you can imagine my parents weren't well pleased at all and tried at once to convince them to move out again. Time was of the essence too because, as everyone knows, it is in the nature of mice to have large families, and to continuously add to them, especially once they have found a nice and cosy place to call their own.

At first my parents started to knock on the walls and the door that leads up to the attic at random times of the day and night in the vain hope of startling the mice, and thereby hopefully persuade them to move out again.

But the mice simply ignored all the knocking and the carrying on and made themselves right comfortable by building nests out of old costumes and pillows and books, and of course by eating everything in sight.

By the time they had created a corridor of poo between the camping gear and the boxes with the Halloween paraphernalia, my parents had finally had enough, and decided there and then that as of now sterner measures were called for.

And so, at last, with a heavy heart, my mum went to a local store and bought some mouse and rat poison. But this being my mum, by the time she got back to the car where my dad was waiting for her, she was so upset about the idea of killing the mice, that she barely made it inside the car before she burst into tears.

My dad had to hold and console her for quite some time. And then he took the box with the poison right out of her hands, got out of the car, and returned it to the shop. And that was the end of that bright idea.

The mice had a field day after that! And the situation only got worse.

And so, finally, after another week of listening to the mice running amok in the attic above their weary heads, my parents decided that even though killing was now firmly out of the question, something drastic had to be done, nevertheless.

They researched a lot *on the line* and finally came across a so-called *humane* trap. Not sure why it was called that, because it sure wasn't big enough for a human to squeeze inside.

Anyway, when my parents finally bought the thing, it turned out to be a transparent, just larger than mouse-sized plastic tube, with an opening on one end, and a closed bit at the front where you were meant to put some food down as bait. The theory being, that the mouse in its eagerness to get at the food, would run inside the trap, dislodge the bait and thereby trigger the falling of a little door at the entrance of the trap, which would then slam shut behind the mouse's bottom, thus trapping it safely inside.

This way no harm would come to the mouse – other than the emotional one by way of loss of their new abode – and whoever had set the trap would then be able to safely pick up what had effectively become a mouse carrier and – once safely outside – set its reluctant inhabitant free by manually opening the trap door once more.

However, as with most things in life, this proved to be very much a case of 'easier said than done'.

So up went the trap into the attic, and then my parents began to check every two hours or so to see if any mouse had been tempted to snack. At first nothing much was happening. My parents then tried a wide variety of food to entice the mice into the trap, but it turned out that the mice were quite particular about what they would or wouldn't eat.

Forget cheese for starters, my mum reckons that stuff only works in the movies. Either that, or generations of mice had by now passed down the lore of cheese being synonymous with getting trapped, and therefore had stopped being enamoured with the stuff.

No, this lot was downright discerning in their tastes. In the end it was chocolate covered wafer bars that did the trick. My mum couldn't believe it.

The first mouse my parents caught was very, very scared when she found the door had closed behind her and she couldn't escape. She was even more scared when she saw my parents staring at her. She was a shy little thing, and so she very much froze on the spot and then simply pretended the whole thing wasn't happening.

My parents couldn't believe the trap had worked at last. It was around midnight and both my parents and the mouse were exhausted from their ordeal. My parents because they had checked the trap literally every half hour, and also every time they heard even the slightest sound coming from the attic, and the mouse because she was frightened and had finally run out of ideas for trying to get the trap door to open again.

My mum and dad felt very sorry for the little mouse and didn't want to cause her to shake even more than she already did.

So they both hurriedly put on some coats over their pyjamas, slipped on their wellies, and stepped out into the night, mouse in tube in hand.

As they didn't want to risk her coming back and moving right back in, my parents decided to carry the little mouse all the way up the hill behind our house, well away from home and any other houses.

And so up they went towards the Country Park (178 steps, remember?!), in the middle of the night, in the freezing cold. The further they got, the worse my mum felt about releasing the poor little mouse into the freezing cold night.

The mouse couldn't have cared less. All *she* wanted was to get as far away from this current nightmare as possible.

In the end my mum finally decided on a nice cosy spot in the undergrowth where she deemed it warm enough for the little mouse and asked my dad to open the trap door. No sooner had he done so than the mouse decided it was time to stop pretending the whole thing wasn't happening and took a running leap into the undergrowth.

Seeing this, my mum felt that maybe all would be well after all. But she also still felt rather guilty for depriving the little mouse of a cosy home with lots of things to nibble on in the attic. In fact she felt so guilty, she made sure to leave some of the chocolate covered wafers behind in the bushes, just in case the mouse still felt hungry.

In all honesty I don't believe it was the mouse's intention to EVER return to the spot where she had last been in such a pickle. But it made my mum feel marginally better about the whole thing.

My parents then went home, put the trap back in the attic, went back to bed and fell asleep at last.

However, sometime later… around 2 am in the morning to be precise, they were rudely woken by a clapping type of sound. As in a trap door snapping shut…

My dad looked at my mum, and my mum looked right back at him, both with a pained expression on their face, that clearly stated 'Surely not!' But unfortunately there was nothing to be done about it, but to climb out of bed once more and to check the trap up in the attic.

This time the mouse trap was occupied by a rather fat (or possibly rather pregnant) mouse who kept ramming her bottom against the door that was trapping her tightly against a half-eaten piece of chocolate covered wafer. She stared moodily at my dad as soon his head appeared outside the trap, indicating that she had no interest whatsoever in eating any more of the treacherous snack, and that all she wanted was to GET OUT! NOW!!!

My parents obliged by putting on their coats and wellies AGAIN, and by traipsing once more up the steep hill, all 178 steps, right to the very top with her. They made sure to release the mouse in the exact same spot as the other one, in case she was hoping for a family reunion with the shy little mouse. My mum also made sure she deposited more chocolatey wafers… Just in case…

And then my parents sighed and home they traipsed once more.

My mum and dad did not put the trap back up into the attic again that night, because they simply couldn't face a repeat of the whole experience for a third time. The next morning they also didn't bother with the trap. But come evening, they reluctantly decided to give the experience another go. And lo-and-behold, a few hours into the night, smack, bang, wallop, they caught themselves another mouse. So once more, bleary-eyed, up they went to the attic to collect the trap and its extremely reluctant occupant.

This one was a proper Alpha mouse. And he was FURIOUS!!! In fact he was in such a stinking, foul mood at the indignity of having been tricked, that he tried his best to smash the trap door with his bottom whilst at the same time trying to rip out the front of the trap with his teeth.

By the time my dad picked him up he had thrashed about so much, that the trap was lying half a meter further down from where it had been placed in the first place. He also wasn't scared. Oh no! Not in the slightest! He just kept staring right back at my parents, gnashing his teeth and burrowing them deeply into the plastic, so that to this day the trap is bearing the scars of the encounter.

Luckily for my parents this was the last trip up the hill in the middle of the night. Same spot, same leaving-some-chocolate-covered-wafer-behind routine, and one furiously incensed mouse left the tube AT HIS OWN PACE, never to return again.

And then my parents giggled all the way back home, wondering what the neighbours were thinking of their nightly excursions, clad in their pyjamas and wellies.

Fortunately that was the end of the mice in our attic. Either my parents had gotten them all just in time before they were able to populate the entire place, or word had gotten out that weird stuff tended to happen to anyone daring to live in our house, and as a result of this everyone quickly moved down the road.

At least that's what I reckon happened, because before you know it, my aunties Barbara and Margaret had suddenly acquired a bunch of unwanted furry lodgers, too.

Unfortunately for them, by the time they finally got a chance to talk to my parents about it, who in turn told them about their own adventures of getting rid of *their* lot, the mice had gone forth and multiplied, and so it took my aunties considerably more trips at night than my parents to relocate the unwanted visitors, before peace and quiet once more descended on their home.

My mum still wonders where all the mice ended up in the end, and she really hopes that they all found a nice home together somewhere in the woods.

And whenever my parents, on their way up to the Country Park, happen to pass the spot where they released the mice, they have a quick peek at the undergrowth.

And then they look at each other and smile.

Chapter 5

GRACIE

Another dog that came into my parent's life after I died, was Gracie. She is a little pug and only has one eye, but what she is missing in the eye department she very much makes up in terms of personality. Her parents are friends of my parents. Before they adopted Gracie they had two little black Mini Schnauzer dogs and sometimes my parents and I would run into them when we were all out and about on our respective walks, when they and I were still around on your side of things.

I only vaguely remember barking and trying to get a rise out of them each time we met, but they were WAY too well behaved to meet me on my level.

Anyway, sometime after both of them had died, their parents found Gracie in a rescue centre and adopted her. They found out pretty soon that she is quite a character and knows exactly what she wants. Especially when it comes to FOOD!

I find her really funny and rather like her. My mum says at times she looks like a right little Miss, which is why she calls her Miss Gracie whenever Gracie sports her haughty look. But she really likes her, too. Only, Gracie utterly prefers my dad. My parents found that out when Gracie's parents asked if mine wouldn't mind looking after her when they were busy doing things somewhere else. My parents replied they'd love to, and that's when little Gracie started hanging out with my mum and dad.

The first time she came over, my dad was away for the first few hours of the evening, and as soon as her own dad had delivered Miss Gracie, she went straight upstairs and parked herself on the armrest of my sofa. And ignored my mum. She only came alive when dinner, and later on a treat, was served, but otherwise kept staring rather disdainfully out of the window. She deigned to be stroked though in a very lady-of-the-manor-like way, which had my mum in stitches.

After two hours or so my dad came home, and my mum says that's when Miss Gracie came alive like a diva in a theatre production. She virtually threw herself at my dad as soon as he lay down on the sofa, then belly crawled languorously across his chest and draped herself across him like a living fur rug. All the while throwing my mum poignant looks as if to say 'See, this is what I wanted all along! This is where I belong'. My mum says it was the funniest thing ever.

It was my mum though who took her for a walk the next time Gracie happened to come over for the day. At first Gracie was all up for it and raced up the steps to the top of the East Hill. But once they had arrived there – in fact as soon as she had done her business – she wasn't so sure that this walk suited her any longer.

And so, halfway up the grassy slope that leads towards the Country Park, little Miss Gracie began to feel quite certain that she had done enough walking for the day, and so she decided to sit this one out.

To that end she parked her bottom firmly and decisively on the grass and refused to move it any further. Not an inch. Not any which way.

Unfortunately for her my mum is just as stubborn. And she is also quite used to carrying difficult little dogs around. And so Miss Gracie got herself a rather unrequested lift. She wasn't best pleased about it, but since she didn't have a choice, and also wasn't in the habit of snapping or flashing her teeth like me – she also has an underbite, just like Billy – she figured that in a way this would count as a victory for herself anyway. After all *she* hadn't moved.

My mum simply ignored her displeased stare and just walked on carrying Miss Gracie further up the hill. But after a while her arms began to ache, even though Gracie isn't half as heavy as I used to be. And so she put her down on the grass once more, in the hope that Miss Gracie would miraculously take to walking again.

But oh no, no such thing! Miss Gracie simply parked her bottom once more on the grass. This time with her back to my mum, indicating that in no way, shape or form was she going to take even a single step further in the wrong direction. I.e. away from home.

My mum only laughed and then she picked Miss Gracie up once more. But once again, as soon as she was put down a little further up the hill, Miss Gracie sat down on the grassy slope with a right pinched look on her face and proceeded to gaze glumly into the distance. With her one eye.

That's when my mum decided to change tack and sat down next to her.

And so they both sat. And sat. And sat some more.

And after a *looooong* while of doing nothing else but sit, Miss Gracie finally got thoroughly bored and totally fed up with all the sitting and the waiting, and the getting absolutely nowhere. So she stood up, turned around, and pointed her one eye moodily in my mum's direction, indicating that she had reluctantly and not exactly graciously decided to give walking another go after all.

And that's when they both resumed their walk.

After Gracie no more dogs showed up on my parents' doorstep and things more or less settled back into their normal routine. *Pan Demic* eventually went back to wherever he had come from and stopped bothering most people. Not much else was happening over here either, and that's when I decided it was finally time to find out all I could about the furry siblings I never knew.

Chapter 6

DENIRO

My mum always believed that I had lived before. Partly because she thought that there was just something in my eyes and demeanour that was different from other dogs. But also because she had the sneaking suspicion that I had been my parents' cat in my previous life. She could never be sure, and my lips are firmly sealed, but this is what she thought.

DeNiro was a black cat with a white spot on his throat and two tiny white spots on his hind toes, and yes, he was named after the actor (sorry, Robert, but my mum thought there was something about him that reminded her of you).

Also, she reckoned he looked rather Italian (???)

and therefore needed an Italian name. Of course his name was immediately shortened to DeNi and he ended up having the usual tons of nicknames my parents come up with on a daily basis.

On the day DeNiro appeared on the scene, my parents were living in a terraced house in London where they had rented a room. Their landlord was a big, burly man, who also lived at the property together with his wife and two cats. There were two other lodgers apart from the landlord, his wife and my parents, and although everyone had their own private bedroom, the kitchen, bathrooms and garden were shared by all.

It was a hot summer's day and my parents, who were having a day off work, were lounging around in the back garden on their own.

Unbeknownst to them, earlier that morning, their landlord had been given a kitten by a friend, and he had promptly managed to lose it by leaving the door to the garden ajar, because he somehow didn't realise that you have to keep kittens inside the house for a while so they get to know their new home and therefore know where they live. Otherwise, being independent little mites, they simply wander off and find themselves a different abode that is more to their liking. Or worse, they'll get lost and can't find their way back home.

Anyway, this particular little kitten in question knew exactly what he wanted. And he sure didn't want to live with the big, burly man, who had left him to his own devices in a strange new house that smelled funny. Nor did he fancy living with his two other cats, one of whom was rather fat and lazy.

And so off the little kitten traipsed through the open door out into the garden. But because he was rather tiny still, he didn't get very far, and having tried to scale the fence at the back of the garden for a while without much success, he gave up at long last and, feeling rather sleepy after all the excitement of the morning, found himself a cosy place to nap.

As I said before, my parents were lounging around and relaxing in the back garden when all of a sudden their landlord appeared outside and asked them if they had seen his new kitten anywhere. They hadn't, but my mum remembered that weirdly about an hour or so before, she had *felt* a kitten somehow. Or rather the picture of a black kitten with a white spot on its chest had popped into her head for no apparent reason.

Now, you all know my mum by now and her weird ways, and the sheer fact that their landlord had told my parents about the kitten AFTER she had felt it, made her feel that this was somehow a sign.

So my parents, together with their landlord, began to scour the garden, and would you believe it, they really did find the kitten. Curled up in a flowerpot and fast asleep. And yes, it was black and had a white spot on its chest…

The landlord picked it up and handed it straight to my mum. He wasn't sure what to do with it, which is strange, because he was supposedly used to cats. And then he asked my parents if they wouldn't mind looking after it for a while in their own room, until the kitten was big enough to be left to its own devices.

My parents agreed, but of course the inevitable happened; they looked into the little kitten's eyes, and he looked right back into theirs, and something clicked and they fell in love. He got his new name and moved into my parents' room that very same day.

That first night DeNiro slept curled up on my mum's chest. However, in the dead of the night he got a bit bored and decided to play catch with her eyeballs, which woke my mum up and freaked her out no end. Luckily he only did it that one time.

Come the next morning he got up early, thoroughly checked out the room where he was now living, sharpened his claws on anything in sight, from the curtains to the bed frame to the carpet, played with anything and everything that wasn't nailed down, shredding the back of my dad's underpants and his socks in the process, then found himself an open drawer to have a nap in, and, in other words, made himself right at home.

At first my parents still told themselves that they were only looking after little DeNiro on behalf of their landlord, but of course they were only kidding themselves because it soon became apparent that they really belonged together. Also, rather unfortunately for their landlord, DeNiro had a *looooong* memory, and he had taken an instant and most formidable dislike to the man. And he didn't hold back in demonstrating this at every opportunity either, by hissing and flashing his teeth at him whenever he was anywhere in the vicinity. And he DEFINITELY refused point blank to be touched by him. Sound familiar? Not saying a thing!

DeNiro came to love my parents very, very much and they loved him right back the exact same way. He liked his new room, but he wasn't allowed to roam anymore, because my parents didn't want him to get lost again. So he explored every inch of it and made it his own. He scratched the hell out of the furniture in his continued and never-ending quest to sharpen his claws, and he slept a lot, mainly on my mum's chest and back, on my dad's lap, on the windowsill, and in every open drawer he could find. He loved drawers so much that when he discovered a hidden one under my parents' bed, he ripped a hole into the fabric at the side of the bed frame so he could get inside it even when the drawer wasn't open.

My parents nearly had a heart attack when they came home one day and couldn't find DeNiro anywhere. They searched and searched but he was nowhere to be found. It really scared them to death and they didn't know what to think and do. Then, all of a sudden, in the middle of the frantic and panicky commotion, a sleepy DeNiro emerged from the hole in the fabric purring loudly and extremely happy to greet them. My parents felt faint with relief, and DeNiro went back to his new favourite hidey-hole. He loved it so much that he used it incessantly until he became too big to squeeze through the hole he had made.

For the first two weeks they were looking after him, my parents kept DeNiro confined to their room and he was only allowed outside by way of being carried in their arms. And as I said, every time he was presented to their landlord, he hissed and spat and made it crystal clear that even though my parents didn't know it yet, he VERY MUCH had decided who his real family were. And it sure as hell didn't include the man he despised with a vengeance.

My parents were quite embarrassed about his rude behaviour and invented a lot of excuses for why this was happening. But come week three, the landlord finally gave my parents an ultimatum: either give DeNiro back at once or adopt him with all the consequences, i.e. the feeding and the vet bills, and the caring for and being responsible for an animal for the rest of its life.

My mum had a good cry about it at first because she was so worried that they couldn't adequately care for him, seeing that my parents' life was quite up and down financially due to the fact that they both worked in the Arts. She was also really scared of taking on this huge responsibility nobody had planned for. She says it was a bit like suddenly finding out that you are pregnant.

But such is life with all its turns and surprises, as my dad pointed out, and then he assured my mum that they would manage. And as he dried her tears, DeNiro made himself right comfortable on the bed, purring all the while. He had no such doubts and he simply knew that my parents loved him very, very much and could never give him up.

But he didn't forgive the landlord for making my mum cry either. And so, after he was officially theirs, and my parents allowed him to roam the rest of the house at last, DeNiro finally got his revenge.

At the first opportunity he got, he wandered down the hallway and pushed open the door leading to the landlord's own bedroom that had been left slightly ajar, confidently strutted inside, pointedly ignored the other two cats who were sleeping side by side on a beanbag, and proceeded to pee at length into the landlord's motorcycle helmet that had been left lying upside down on the floor. Which was no mean feat because it kept wobbling about an awful lot.

Nobody saw and was none the wiser, but come the next morning the landlord was in a great rush to get to work. So he hastily showered, quickly got dressed, put on his jacket and shoes, grabbed his keys and bag, and... um... put on his motorcycle helmet...

At least that's what my parents figured had happened, because next thing they knew, their landlord came running down the hallway, pounded on their bedroom door and shouted something about putting on his helmet and feeling something warm and smelly dripping all over his hair and shoulders. Something that very much smelled like pee, and clearly hadn't been in his motorcycle helmet before. And since his own two placid cats would never DARE to do something like this, he was sure who the culprit had to be.

And before you ask, no, DeNiro NEVER peed

anywhere inside either, apart from in his litter box. Which is why both my parents and the landlord knew for a fact that the act had been deliberate. And, according to the landlord, malicious. My parents of course denied all knowledge and tried their very hardest not to burst out laughing before they could close their bedroom door behind him. And my mum says, during all this DeNiro sat on the bed with a decidedly smug expression on his face.

Unfortunately, after that little incident things became rather awkward around the house as my parents' relationship with their landlord had become decidedly frosty.

DeNiro, though, continued to have a whale of a time with my parents, and they with him, and things only got better after they all finally moved house to avoid any future embarrassments. Among other reasons.

Every day brought new adventures, and they were all as close as you can possibly get to someone you love. DeNiro had an extra special bond with my mum and dad, and he always knew the precise moment when either of them would come home from work.

He would always stop whatever he was doing, stride to the front door and wait for them there until they opened the door. Then he would loudly greet them, get some cuddles, and if my mum ever overdid it with her many *mimos*, he would grab her nostril with his teeth and squeeze a bit whilst looking her firmly in the eyes, to make sure she got the message that enough was enough already.

My mum says DeNiro was incredibly intelligent. And headstrong. And if he wanted something or was displeased you would know about it. She remembers that he once slapped a visiting friend on the shoulder HARD because she happened to have her back to him while talking to my mum. And then he positively grinned at her when she screeched in fright and swivelled around to find him sitting on the kitchen worktop behind her.

DeNiro also never stopped to learn new things (and tricks) by observing what humans did all the time and copying them afterwards. He gave brushing his teeth a miss, though, even though he watched my parents like a hawk whenever they brushed theirs, because he could never quite figure out why on earth they would bother doing it.

My mum in turn learned how to purr from DeNiro. She got really good at it, too. Problem was, she then forgot herself and started to purr in public. Whenever she came across a cat somewhere outside, she would purr instead of talking to it. Startled quite a few of them, I can tell you!

Then, one evening, as she was walking past a house in the neighbourhood, she spotted a cat at the end of a long front garden and, believing herself to be alone and completely unobserved, began to purr as loudly as she possibly could over the garden fence in the direction of the cat.

Unfortunately… she wasn't alone… as she found out to her huge embarrassment when the owner of the house, who she hadn't spotted before, suddenly moved. She later told my dad he had looked at her as if she'd completely lost her marbles.

And as my mum hurriedly left the scene with her face the colour of a ripe tomato, she promised herself not to *ever* walk down that street again.

She didn't do much more purring in public after that. But she *did* purr at me once. Didn't go down too well either – had to snarl at her to make her stop.

My parents and DeNiro definitely had a lot of good times during all the years they spent together. And okay, there were bad times too, because that's what happens in life – like the time when DeNiro got lost, and when he came back, he had contracted, what the vet later told my mum and dad was *Feline AIDS*, from the many fights he had to fight with other cats while he was gone. But nobody knew it at first, and by the time they found out it was way too late and nothing could be done about it.

But on the whole DeNiro's life with my parents was full of love, adventure and fun.

I won't tell you how DeNiro died because it upsets my mum an awful lot and I don't want to make her cry again. Suffice to say that she really broke down when he did.

My mum was playing the lead role in a play at the time, but since the theatre was small and she didn't have an understudy, she couldn't just stay at home and grieve. No, she had to perform every night for weeks on end, and sometimes twice a day, even though her heart was breaking into a thousand tiny pieces silently inside of her.

She had to stand on stage and act and laugh and sing and entertain the audience. And each night afterwards she would go back to where she was staying for the duration of the play and cry and be violently sick. All night long. She lost a lot of weight during that time. And at last the director of the play took her to see a doctor because he wanted him to give my mum some pills to calm her down. But, my mum says, luckily for her this doctor was very old-school and wise. He took one look at her and said 'Unfortunately there is no pill against grief. Only time can heal it.' And he was right.

It took an awful long time though, but DeNiro did send my parents lots of messages to let them know that he was still around. He got really good at it, too.

At the time my parents were still living in London, and on the first floor of their house there was a special little area, right on the landing between two rooms, which my mum and dad had filled with shelves and rows upon rows of books. This little library didn't have any doors or windows and was therefore completely sheltered from any drafts. I'm only telling you this because my parents say that it proves that there was no other explanation for what happened next, other than DeNiro sending them a message.

On one of the shelves, my parents had placed a photo of DeNiro (without a frame), right next to another one of my brother Alfred, the Scottie dog, who they had also adopted by then.

Now, whenever my mum got terribly upset about DeNiro not being around any longer, next thing you knew, the photo of DeNiro would be lying in the middle of the library, face up on the floor. Every single time. And it had never done that before, in all the years my parents lived there, when DeNiro was still alive.

My parents reckon that if the photo had just fallen down by accident, or blown off the shelf by a draft, chances are that it wouldn't have ended up in the exact same spot in the exact same way, time after time after time.

Also, the photo of Alfred that was located right next to DeNiro's NEVER found its way to the floor. Not even once.

My parents took great comfort from the messages DeNiro sent them, and they really treasured them.

And still do.

Chapter 7

NEFERTITI

… AND A LOT MORE OF DENIRO…

Nefertiti's story begins with DeNiro, because he was the one who found her when he was lost.

As DeNiro grew bigger, my parents started to take him everywhere. Even on holidays. At the time they owned a small motorhome that had been their home for a little while when they first explored the UK. They took DeNiro on a trip in it too, and he used to sleep and sunbathe on the dashboard whenever they stopped driving. He was so happy going places with my parents that they decided to take him with them when a friend asked them to house-, cat- and dog-sit for her over Christmas one year.

But unfortunately that's when it became

apparent that DeNiro was a bit of an escape artist. Which earned him the nickname *Houdini.* My mum says he was highly independent and always knew exactly what he wanted and especially what he *didn't* want. And so, on day two of their stay, when DeNiro was safely locked inside the room my parents were staying in at their friend's house so he couldn't abscond, he decided what he definitely did NOT want was to stay at home alone in this boring old room, and that it was in fact high time he went outside on a recce.

That was the first time DeNiro vanished. My parents came back from walking their friend's dogs and found him gone. The bedroom door was still closed, but on closer inspection the window that had been closed before was now slightly ajar, even though my mum and dad were sure no one had opened it.

At the time they couldn't explain it, but of course, a few months later they found out that DeNiro had somehow managed to teach himself to open windows, because they caught him red-pawed in the act, and therefore later deduced that he must have opened the window and somehow leapt down two storeys in his haste to get into the back garden and away from their friend's Persian cats who he didn't consider to be proper cats at all.

In fact, DeNiro became such a prolific window opener that he ended up with a permanent scar over his nose from where he would use it to unhook the sharp-edged metal window fastening.

And how did my parents eventually find out he could do it? Well, during the time they all still lived in the shared house in London, DeNiro was only allowed to roam the house and garden when my parents were at home, too. But when they were away working or were home but didn't think it was safe for him to go outside, they would close all the windows and doors and lock him into their bedroom.

Now, DeNiro had gotten into the habit of exiting through the French doors of the downstairs communal kitchen into the garden, but not to come back the same way. Instead, he would reappear on the roof outside my parents' first floor bedroom window begging to be let in again. And since he could only do so if someone had opened the French doors or a window for him, my parents became very suspicious when DeNiro suddenly appeared outside their window on days when they were sure nobody else was in the house and none of the doors or windows had been left open.

At first they thought maybe they had been careless, or that maybe someone else in their shared household had inadvertently left the window open, but then they noticed a little cut just above DeNiro's nose that bled, then healed, then bled again. And they also noticed that the metal latch in the downstairs bathroom hadn't been hooked in properly to prevent the opened window from swaying in the wind.

And so they finally put two and two together. And didn't believe what they came up with at all, because they figured there was simply NO WAY DeNiro could have figured out how the rather complex window opening process worked. In other words, they totally underestimated him. Nothing new there. Humans can be so arrogant sometimes. Honestly!

Anyway. Since it kept happening, my parents decided to properly investigate at last. And so one day they secretly followed DeNiro downstairs and saw him enter the downstairs bathroom. When they quickly followed him inside to see what he was up to, DeNiro was sitting on the windowsill trying his hardest to look innocent.

My mum says if he had been human he would probably have whistled or drummed his fingers, or sung 'La la la' or something. As he was a cat he did what cats do when they want to distract any pesky humans around – he began to clean himself. Extensively and with a rather bored look on his face as if to say 'Look, I'm just doing my usual thing. Nothing special going on here at all.'

But as soon as my mum and dad had left the bathroom again, he went straight back to what he had come down to do in the first place – i.e. to open the window.

Only this time he had been tricked into believing he was unobserved because my parents were secretly watching him through a gap in the door. And to their utter amazement they watched him deftly open the window like a pro, which was no mean feat since the window didn't only have a handle but also a metal safety latch, both of which needed to be not only lifted but also pushed, and all in the right sequence.

But DeNiro being DeNiro, managed to accomplish this in less than a minute, and then he proudly strutted out into the garden. My parents COULD NOT BELIEVE IT!

And that's when it dawned on them that he must have done the same thing to escape from their friend's bedroom window the Christmas before.

What followed DeNiro's escapade at that time were two days of frantically searching for him until my parents' friend, who by now had come back from her holidays, had the bright idea to bribe him back by standing in the back garden with a chicken drumstick in her hand and cooing his name.

Luckily by the time she came up with the idea, DeNiro was hungry as a wolf, and so he reappeared from wherever he had been, grabbed the drumstick, my parents' friend grabbed him in turn, and then she returned him safely to my hysterical and very relieved parents.

After that the vet told my parents that DeNiro's thirst for exploration had nothing to do with wanting to leave home, it was because he had not been neutered and he therefore had this big hormonal urge to find a mate. He tried to explain to my parents that for a tomcat in a big city it wasn't nice at all not to be neutered because it didn't mean that he *could* mate, but that he HAD to. And with all the competition around that would mean constant fighting, constantly being attacked and hurt, and constantly being on the prowl whenever a female cat in the vicinity was in heat.

But my parents didn't want to know, because they loved DeNiro *soooo* much, just the way he was, and they didn't want to change him in any way. *Biiiiiig* mistake!

Because just a little while later my mum and dad decided to move into a small bedsit in a large Victorian house, and the first thing DeNiro did was to escape once more. And this time he didn't remember his way back home. Because he hadn't been long enough at the new place to mark it properly in his frantic urge to find the cat whose smell had made him run for miles to find her.

What followed were four eternally long and horrible months during which my parents combed the neighbourhood by day and night and my mum cried herself to sleep each night. And she also kept imploring the empty air around her 'Please let him come back! Please, please, PLEASE!!' Over and over again.

My mum later said it was the not knowing that made things so much worse to bear. Because when someone dies you somehow have to deal with it and come to terms with it because you know it's final, but when the person you love vanishes you can never move on, because you can never allow yourself to give up hope that they might come back one day. And then you worry yourself sick all the time not knowing if they are suffering and what is happening to them.

One of the things my parents did in their desperation to find DeNiro was to inform the local police that he had gone missing. Just in case someone had handed him in. Weird, I know, but my mum says it was the time before you could do all the things you can do now *on the line* to find someone.

After that my parents also called the vet and all the charities and animal rescue organisations they could think of.

Sometime during doing all this someone

mentioned a local lady called Mrs Foley, who was known for taking in strays, cats and dogs alike, and they told my parents to contact her for help. And so they did.

Mrs Foley came over the same day, my mum cried on her shoulder for a longish while, but unfortunately Mrs Foley hadn't seen DeNiro either. But she promised to keep an eye out just in case.

After that nothing much happened, but as I told you before, four long, horrible months passed by, but my mum and dad refused to give up hope.

And then something incredible happened. One day, out of the blue, my mum got a phone call from Mrs Foley, who unbelievably also had never forgotten DeNiro even though she had never met him, and only had met my parents once.

Mrs Foley told my mum that she had taken some stray cats to the vet's to be neutered. Whilst waiting to see the vet she got chatting to a lady in the seat next to her. And can you believe it, she actually asked this lady whether she had seen DeNiro. She even remembered the description my mum had given her. After all this time!

And even more incredibly the lady said yes, she thought she had. A very battered and emaciated tomcat that nevertheless fitted DeNiro's description had come into her back garden almost every evening for months on end, and the lady had started to feed it because she felt sorry for it. She told Mrs Foley that the tomcat had accepted the food gratefully, but that even after all this time it wouldn't let her stroke or touch it at all. In fact it wouldn't let ANYONE touch it – you can't see this, but I'm smiling over here...

And after the tomcat had come over for a month or so, it had started to bring a tiny female, black kitten along with it which it fiercely protected from all the other cats in the area.

When my mum heard all this she started to shake all over. She and my dad wanted to rush over to where the lady lived right there and then. But Mrs Foley told them they would have to be patient and wait until the tomcat was back to feed in the lady's back garden at which point she would call them immediately. My mum says although only two days passed after that it was the longest wait ever. She also didn't want to get her hopes up too high just in case it turned out the tomcat wasn't DeNiro after all.

By the time the call finally came, my mum was a nervous wreck. And my dad wasn't much better either. And guess what, it happened to be another Wednesday! In case you don't remember or don't know yet, for some strange reason important things always seem to be happening on a Wednesday in my family. It's the weirdest thing. I died on a Wednesday, too, if you remember, and so did my Grandma Olga. I mean, what is it with Wednesdays and my family??!!

Anyway, on this particular Wednesday, my

dad was still out working, but Mrs Foley rushed over to lend support. My mum quickly grabbed her bags and DeNiro's travel carrier, just in case the tomcat turned out to be really him, and together with Mrs Foley hurriedly left the house. She didn't have far to go because ironically the house where the tomcat came to feed turned out to be only three streets further down from where my parents lived.

As soon as my mum and Mrs Foley got there, they hurried through the house to the back garden, because everyone was worried that the tomcat once fed would disappear again. Luckily for my mum's extremely frayed nerves that was not the case.

When she got to the back garden, my mum took one look at the cat, and then she literally dropped to her knees and started to bawl.

Because sometimes in life wishes do come true, and it really was DeNiro who finally and against all the immense odds had been found.

He recognised my mum immediately, too and came over to her when she called out to him, but he seemed to be in shock. As if he couldn't quite believe that he had finally found his mum again. Maybe he thought he was dreaming and didn't want to believe that the hellish time he had had was finally over, and he was treading carefully because he didn't want to wake up.

DeNiro was in a very bad state; part of his ear was missing, he had an abscess and multiple bloody scratches on his face, some of his claws were broken off, and he positively REEKED of pee. But my mum just didn't care. As soon as he was close enough she grabbed him, buried her face deeply in his smelly fur, and then she held him tight and promised him she would never let him go again.

In fact, she held him so tight that he began to find it hard to breathe and had to mewl to let her know. But he also started to purr. My mum says at first it was only a broken little purr as if he hadn't purred in a long, long time. But then he really got into it because he was just so relieved that he was finally back with the people he loved more than anyone in the world.

Both my parents say they can never, ever thank Mrs Foley enough, because if it hadn't been for her and the kind lady who fed DeNiro, they would never have been reunited.

Later that day, when my dad finally came home from work and got his chance to hug and kiss the still VERY smelly DeNiro, my parents discussed the little kitten DeNiro had protected during his absence, and they were very worried what would happen to her without him now.

And yes – you could see this one coming a mile

away – OF COURSE they came to the only logical conclusion. They simply couldn't leave her behind, all alone and at the mercy of the other strays out there.

And that's how my parents came to adopt the little kitten. Even though they only lived in a small bedsit, where literally everything, including the kitchen, was in the same room, apart from the bathroom which was shared with all the other people in the house. It was crowded but they made do. Little did they know that it would soon become even more crowded when my dad would find and rescue Alfred, the Scottie dog. But I'll tell you his story in a moment.

The other thing my mum and dad agreed upon that day was that the vet had been right all along, and that both DeNiro and the kitten needed to be neutered after all. Of course they still worried a lot about whether this would change DeNiro's personality and demeanour.

But they needn't have worried at all. As soon as he had the snip and came back home after the op, he humped the first female cat he came across. And then looked pointedly at my mum and dad.

When my parents told the vet about it, he chuckled a lot, and then he said that it probably had something to do with his Italian genes…

Oh, and of course having been neutered didn't change DeNiro's character. Not one single bit. His personality was WAY too big for that.

And the kitten? Well, the kitten was small, very slim and sleek and completely black. She was called Nefertiti, and really looked Egyptian too, but for once this wasn't a name my mum had come up with. The lady who had found DeNiro had bestowed it on her. But my mum thought it suited the little cat, and so my parents kept the name. However, since my mum and dad also couldn't quite see themselves standing in the back garden in the middle of the night shouting 'Nefertiti' or 'Where are you, Nefertiti?', or worse still 'Nefertiti, come on in!' and thereby confirming to the next-door neighbours once and for all just how nutty my parents were, her name got swiftly shortened to Neffie and stayed that way until she died.

Neffie was a very skittish little cat and lived very much in the shadow of her brother DeNiro. Once my parents had bought and moved into their first house, she always stayed upstairs and rarely went downstairs or outside. My parents put this down to her being painfully shy, but strangely as soon as DeNiro had died she suddenly started to venture downstairs all the time, which made my mum wonder if it hadn't been DeNiro who had ordered her to stay upstairs and out of sight because, although he had rescued her, he still very much wanted my parents all to himself.

But even after DeNiro's death Neffie was never completely comfortable with being the centre of attention. But there was one person in her life who she loved an awful lot. That person was her Uncle Jack. Uncle Jack had lived in the same house where my parents used to rent their bedsit, and he and my parents had become fast friends during the years they lived there. So they stayed in touch even after my parents bought their first house, and Uncle Jack swiftly became the designated cat (and later also dog) sitter for when my parents weren't around. But whereas DeNiro would be quite aloof during those times, because he was very choosy with who was allowed to touch him and when... ahem..., Neffie simply *looooved* having her favourite uncle around. And Uncle Jack loved her very much, too. With him she could finally be herself, and she loved all the stroking and the many cuddles she got. And she stayed very close to him until the day she died.

Right up until that moment though, Neffie very much enjoyed the quieter moments in life, like staying inside and snoozing in the sunshine after a nice meal – especially on the guest bed upstairs where no dogs were allowed to go.

And not having to worry about a single thing.

Chapter 8

ALFRED

My brother Alfred was a Scottie dog. If you have read my own story you will probably remember the story about him and the fox. Well, here are a few bits that you don't yet know.

Around the time when my parents still lived in their bedsit together with DeNiro and Neffie, Alfred had been bought and taken away from his birth family by what turned out to be two really heartless people, who one summer's day only a few months later, when Alfred was still only a puppy, decided to throw him out of their home without another thought and abandon him to his fate on the streets of London. He had a horrible time out there trying desperately to fend for himself, but luckily for Alfred my dad found and rescued him from certain death just in time. I once dictated the whole story of his life to my mum. It's called *'My Brother Alfred'* – well, it would be, wouldn't it?! Alfred's story is a bit sad, but fortunately it had a happy ending. My parents adopted him and the already rather crowded bedsit henceforth housed two humans, two cats *and* one dog.

Do you remember that I once told you that my mum invents new names for people she loves pretty much all of the time? Oh yes, she does! And then she will call you that new name for a while and change it again a few days – or months – later. But of course we all know our real names and just ignore her when she does it. Only Billy was saved from having endless nicknames on end because he doesn't live permanently with my mum and dad. Mind you, come to think of it, I *did* hear my mum utter *Groucho* under her breath on more than one occasion when Billy's eyebrows and moustache were all fluffed up after yet another shower.

Anyway, in the case of Alfred my mum had twelve years of entertainment in coming up with ever new nicknames. Some names made sense, like… *Roble* for example. That's Spanish for oak tree and was quite fitting because Alfred *was* really sturdy and earth bound, but also because whenever he had the misfortune of being picked up by anyone, he would immediately spread out his legs in all directions in his utter panic at having been separated from solid ground. Which made him look as if he had sprouted branches all of a sudden. According to my mum, he then looked – and felt – positively uprooted with all his legs sticking out at odd angles.

Some names however made only *sort of* sense, like… *Donkeyman.* Poor old Alfred got lumbered with that particular name because my mum swore blind that his face had a certain resemblance to that of a donkey – and even my dad had to agree that it did.

But most names my mum came up with didn't really make any sense. AT ALL.

One time she insisted on calling Alfred *Carruthers* for days on end. When asked by someone as to why, she argued that he looked like one???!!!

I rest my case.

But Alfred didn't really mind all the different names because he knew that my mum only gave them to him because she loved him.

Someone else who loved my brother Alfred from the start, was Uncle Vini. So much so that when Alfred died, Uncle Vini was determined never to get close to another dog ever again out of respect for him. Which is why he tried his very best to ignore me on the day I was introduced to him for the first time.

But of course he hadn't counted with me. And so, when I jumped up onto the sofa next to him and first licked his hand, and then his face, and then his whole shiny, smooth head, he simply couldn't help himself. He laughed, and then he stroked me, and we were super close after that.

Oh, and I really don't think Alfred minded one single bit. Like I said before, once you're over here you understand and really *get* things in a different way.

I may have mentioned that Alfred was on the whole very placid and sleepy, but when it came to other dogs he was a right little fiend due to what had happened to him as a puppy, when he had been attacked by some dogs during the time when he was lost on the streets of London before my dad found and rescued him. Alfred REALLY hated other dogs with a vengeance and that feeling only grew and got worse as he got older.

He would run at them and bark and bark and BARK, and nothing and no one could stop or shut him up. So in the end my mum decided it was time to take him to doggie training classes to try and change his behaviour.

She enrolled him in a group class run by a very experienced dog trainer and took him there once a week on a Thursday afternoon. However, it soon became apparent that Alfred made a BIG distinction between indoor and outdoor behaviour. My mum tried telling the trainer that at the vet's Alfred tended to ignore other dogs because he was indoors, and probably too scared to have a go at them without an open escape route in case they retaliated. But his behaviour in the park or on the street was an entirely different matter.

The trainer completely dismissed what my mum had said and told her that it didn't matter, and that by teaching Alfred to 'Sit!' and 'Lie down!' and 'Fetch!' in the company of other dogs, he would soon come around and lose his aggressive behaviour.

My mum was doubtful to say the least but decided to give it a go. Alfred also decided to give it a go. After all there were lots of treats to be had. Without having to endure any cuddles in exchange for them. Because he wasn't too fond of them either.

And so he learned to sit (most of the time) and

lie down (occasionally) and to fetch (not so much). He was literally on his best behaviour every Thursday afternoon, he ignored all the other dogs in the room, and one day, during a competition, he even won the rosette for 'Perfect Recall' together with my mum.

And then the class was over and Alfred went outside and tried to murder every dog in sight.

And that was the end of the doggie training classes. My mum figured it was a complete waste of time, money and treats.

Yep, Alfred won that round paws down, and he stayed true to his character until the day he died.

Alfred wasn't too keen on cats either, but since they were in charge and part of his family, he accepted them – not that he really had a choice in the matter.

He never tried to chase them and stayed well out of their way, and only once retaliated when whacked in the face by Neffie for no reason other than that she happened to be in a foul mood that day. She only did it the once because she sported a smarting bump for a while after the encounter because Alfred bit her just above the eye to make sure she would never do it again. And for most of the time thereafter they were civil when they ran into each other but not exactly on speaking terms either.

Funnily enough though, Alfred did accept his brother Oscar, the Jack Russell, when my parents adopted him into the household a little while later. He only nipped him once, my mum and dad objected loudly, and that was the end of it.

Oscar, or Ossie, as he was known, never forgot or forgave him though, and one day, when Alfred accidentally got locked out in the garden, he finally got his own back. And so as Alfred pleadingly looked at Ossie through the French glass doors, imploring him to raise the alarm with my parents, Ossie stared straight back at Alfred and then slowly and pointedly turned his back on him, lay back in his basket and went to sleep.

And poor old Alfred, who, as I told you before, had a major problem with being anything but polite and rather hesitant in showing some character, only stood there forlornly in front of the French doors without barking once, until some four hours later my dad spotted him by accident and opened the door to let him back in.

On the whole though Alfred and Ossie got on, even though Alfred never understood his new brother completely. He especially couldn't believe that Ossie would dare to try to break all the house rules pretty much all of the time. Rules such as 'Don't go upstairs! or 'Don't wipe your dirty paws or bottom on the sofa!'. Because in his later years Alfred followed rules quite happily and really came to like them too, since they gave his life constancy and structure. Ossie on the other hand dismissed rules. *And* Alfred. And then he pretended that he was an only dog.

Alfred and Ossie had very different routines, too. Alfred would prefer to lie in his own bed or on the living room rug next to my dad by the sofa, as far away from my mum's many *mimos* as possible, whereas Ossie really loved cuddling up to her, preferably under the blanket when they were both lying on the sofa. He even wriggled himself under her jumper or jacket just so he could be as close to her as possible. In fact Ossie loved being inside blankets and under woollen throws so much, that my parents decided to wrap him up in his favourite blanket and bury him in the back garden after he had died.

Unfortunately they made the mistake of showing his little dead body to Alfred before they did so because they mistakenly figured that he would want to say goodbye. And also because they wanted Alfred to understand why Ossie wouldn't be around any longer.

But all a panicky Alfred understood was that Ossie was clearly dead, and when he saw my mum wrapping him in his favourite blanket and my dad digging a grave in the back garden he completely freaked out because he thought that they had murdered his brother and were getting rid of the evidence. He hid in the living room at once and avoided them both like the plague for a few weeks until he could be sure they wouldn't be doing the same to him, too.

He preferred to stay with Uncle Vini and Auntie Dee for a while after that, especially since Uncle Vini was always ready to share his dinner with him. In this alone, he and I were alike, we both liked to hang out with Uncle Vini a lot and not only because you could always get some extra bits of food.

Auntie Dee though was less enamoured with Alfred because he would always get between her legs when she was cooking, and silently and intently stare at her until dinner was served. She felt it was disconcerting and ever so slightly creepy. Especially since he would duck whenever she wanted to touch or cuddle him, then sidestep and go back to staring at her until finally some food was forthcoming.

Eventually though Alfred got over his fear of being murdered and life went back to normal. My parents sold their house in London and moved down to the South Coast pretty soon afterwards, taking Alfred with them.

Being rather partial to his creature comforts, Alfred very much hoped the new house would have soft carpets throughout for a change, but unfortunately for him, no sooner had he clapped eyes on the comfy, shaggy carpets of his new home-to-be, than my parents ripped them out to expose the wooden floor beneath. He wasn't best pleased about it, I can tell you, but unlike me he didn't make a fuss, and kept his displeasure to himself.

But on the whole Alfred came to like his new abode. He also really appreciated the fresher air by the sea, and like me he *loooved* his many walks through the Country Park. My parents enjoyed them less, because there were always lots of other dogs about in the park, and since Alfred hadn't lost his intense hatred of them, everyone always heard them coming a mile away.

As soon as Alfred spotted a dog, even far, far away in the distance, he would majorly let rip. And believe me, he had a VERY LOUD, INSISTENT BARK! And there was no distracting him. Not with food. Not with pleading. Not with shouting. Not with anything!

My mum says there was only turning around and dragging Alfred away, and apologising A LOT to the people whose dog inadvertently had caused Alfred to start the whole mighty ruckus.

Knowing this was what would happen whenever Alfred came across another dog, my parents eventually came up with an evasive routine to avoid the whole drama. It involved one of them quickly picking up Alfred whenever they happened to spot a dog before *he* did, and the other one covering Alfred's eyes with their hands until they had passed said dog. This manoeuvre would successfully distract Alfred who, although he could smell the other dog, despite frantically blinking against my mum or dad's hand, wouldn't be able to see it and therefore would keep *shtum*. Ish…

As soon as his eyes were uncovered once more, Alfred would stop dead and stare into the distance in utter disbelief, because he simply couldn't comprehend that he couldn't see what his nose clearly told him must be there.

Luckily for my parents, he would never turn around to check what was going on behind him after they had put him down again, because once Alfred was pointed in one direction, that tended to be generally the direction he would proceed in.

That's also how he once ended up in a pond.

My parents had taken him to Cornwall on holiday where they had rented a cottage together with some friends. Upon arrival Alfred needed to pee, so my dad let him out into the back garden. Which means he was pointed in the direction of the bottom of the garden.

So Alfred did his usual thing and slowly started to trot, trotted some more, all in a straight line down the garden path, gained a lot of momentum doing so, then couldn't stop to save his life – forget swerving, too – and thus ploughed head first into the pond at the end of the garden. Came out the other end looking like a sea monster, all covered in seaweed and other slimy stuff. Stank mightily, too. My mum says he was a right sight, and it took her and my dad ages to get all the gunk out of his fur.

Apart from the rows with other dogs and the inconvenience of having mostly wooden floors, Alfred enjoyed his new quieter life by the sea. Not so much the sea itself, though, because he didn't like to get his paws wet. And not the beach either come to think of it. I mean, he would have liked it had it not been full of pebbles. As things were, he was relegated to gingerly putting one careful step in front of the other and wobble about like a drunk, with a pained look on his face because his sensitive paws were hurting. So, no racing about for him, like I used to do. No game of 'find that pebble' either. Only looking for the closest exit. And sighing a very audible sigh of relief when he was back on the paved road leading to the beach.

But on the whole Alfred had a good time that last year of his life with my parents. He was the last dog standing so to speak, before I came along, having survived all his other furry siblings. And even though he didn't *really* like being the centre of attention, since that meant having to endure my mum's endless cuddles as there was no one left to share them with, he thoroughly enjoyed finally having his bed and living room rug wholly to himself.

I asked Alfred what had happened to him right at the end of his life, but as I once told you, he didn't want to talk about how he got over here. He still doesn't. He wants to keep the good memories.

And that's okay by me.

Chapter 9

OSCAR

My brother Oscar and my parents found each other in a rather special way. I reckon you could say that it was very much a case of all of them being exactly in the right place at the right time.

On a lovely spring day, roughly two years after DeNiro had died, my dad took my mum for a walk through Greenwich Park to take her mind off things. My mum was still heart-broken over the death of DeNiro even though two whole years had passed, and she refused point-blank to ever adopt another cat again. Not that my parents really wanted to do that anyway since they still had Neffie (and Alfred) and felt that the family was quite big enough.

The sun was shining and my parents were strolling along aimlessly for a while until sometime later they came across the Pavilion Café, right up on the hill overlooking Greenwich, and decided to stop for some tea and coffee. Once inside, they chatted a lot about this and that, as they always do, but looking back on it later, I heard them tell someone that they both vividly recall talking specifically about the loss of DeNiro and how they would find it impossible to replace him by adopting another cat, but that adopting another dog instead wasn't really their thing either because, as they put it, 'deep down they were really cat and not dog people'.

Ha ha ha, famous last words!

Because literally only a few minutes later, right after my parents had left the café and were continuing on their walk, they came across a market at the bottom of the hill, where a market stall holder was selling his wares, a little tan coloured Jack Russell dog in a faded basket at his side. And my mum who can never resist the opportunity for a cuddle, immediately bent down to stroke the little dog. And then she famously exclaimed 'Oh, what a lovely, little dog! Now if *he* needed a home, I'd have him!'. To which the market stall holder replied 'Well actually, I am looking for someone to take him because I can't keep him any longer.'

Yep, you couldn't make it up!!!

And that's how my parents ended up adopting a little dog. Minutes after they had proclaimed themselves to be "cat people"… ahem…

The market stall holder told my parents that the little dog was called Oscar, and that he had had a horrible time when he was only a puppy. Apparently, he first belonged to a man who took out his frustration at having ended up in a wheelchair on Oscar and almost beat him to death. Oscar very nearly didn't survive the attack and when he miraculously and against all the odds did, he was crooked because all his bones had knitted back together in a misshapen way, leaving him lop-sided.

He was then rescued by the market stall holder who kept him for a few years, but ultimately felt he couldn't do so any longer because he couldn't take Oscar to work with him. That's because he only sold his wares at the street market, where my mum and dad had met him, on weekends, but during the rest of the week he worked at a place where dogs weren't allowed to enter. But because the market stall holder couldn't leave Oscar at home alone either on account of him howling down the house each time he was left to his own devices, this meant that poor Oscar had to wait endless hours for him in the car in the freezing cold during winter, or in the boiling heat when it was summer. And so the market stall holder finally decided to do the right thing and to give Oscar away rather than have him suffer.

And that's why he offered him to my parents on that fateful day.

Oscar arrived on a Wednesday the week after he had met my parents for the first time. He was only meant to stay for a trial of three days at first, so that my parents could establish if Alfred and Neffie would accept this new addition to the family. Also, my parents wanted to find out whether Uncle Vini and Auntie Dee and some of their other close friends would agree to dog-sit two dogs rather than just one whenever my parents had to go away. And for that they wanted the extended family to meet Oscar first.

When the market stall holder brought Oscar over that Wednesday, my mum and dad met them outside their house together with Alfred to avoid any territory issues, and then they all went on a walk together to see what would happen. And that's when Alfred – who as you know had a MAJOR problem with dogs thanks to his own difficult time as a puppy – nipped him once, my mum and dad firmly told him off for it, and weirdly after that Alfred simply gave up and didn't object to Oscar's presence any longer.

Maybe Alfred was in a mellow mood that day, or maybe he knew deep down that Oscar badly needed rescuing, but as a result of this he got himself a brand new brother.

When they all got back to the house after their walk and my dad opened the front door, Oscar marched straight in and down the corridor, without the slightest hesitation, all the way through the kitchen too, and straight out the other end into the garden, via the cat flap, which amused my parents no end.

He left a startled Alfred in his wake, because all *he* could fit through the cat flap was his shaggy head. And believe me he tried to push the rest of himself through on many occasions in the following years when Oscar had exited through the cat flap once more.

My mum says the funny thing was that Oscar very much seemed to think that the cat flap was a one-way street. He would only use it on his way out, and after he had done his business on the lawn, he would return, pointedly turn his back on the cat flap and bark for someone to open the back door for him. He would bark just the once, then pause, and if nobody reacted immediately he would bark again. Single barks each time, but louder and louder after each pause, still not deigning to turn around as this would have indicated urgency and therefore weakness, and he very much wanted everyone to believe that he couldn't have cared less. But with an increasingly indignant look on his face that clearly stated 'You just can't get the staff these days!'.

He had my parents well trained in no time at all. For the longest time they thought the poor thing just couldn't manage to get back in by himself because of his crooked back. This was only proven to be a complete and utter lie when Grandma C came over from Germany to stay with my parents for a few weeks. During that time my parents were very busy working elsewhere, and so it fell to Grandma C to look after the house and everyone in it. But unfortunately for Oscar, who by then was mostly known as Ossie, Grandma C wasn't my parents, and she sure didn't consider herself to be at the beck and call of one grumpy little Jack Russell with the attitude of the lord of the manor.

My parents never found out if Grandma C forgot or simply ignored Ossie's barking commands for the back door to be opened, but one way or the other said door never got opened. And so in an almighty huff, Ossie finally gave up and made his entrance back through the cat flap on his own, thus proving once and for all that he was very much capable of doing so in the first place.

And yes, Grandma C told my parents about it. Which meant that from that moment on everyone simply ignored Ossie's demands, and he had to get in and out of the door by himself. He was most annoyed about the whole thing and he made his displeasure known every single time he entered the house from the garden by throwing filthy looks at whoever saw him do so.

But let me go back to the day when Oscar first arrived at his new home. After his sprint to the back garden, Ossie came back inside and proceeded to explore the rest of the house. Alfred followed him around as he did so, but he very much stayed on his best behaviour.

But Neffie, hair standing on end, quickly took herself upstairs as soon as she spotted Ossie and then ignored him, and as Ossie wasn't allowed to follow, he ignored her right back.

After that the market stall holder left. He didn't say goodbye to Ossie and Ossie didn't say goodbye to him. I think they both wanted to avoid any painful scenes. And Ossie just wanted to get on with his new life.

After the three days of the trial were over and all my parents' friends had met him and had promised to look after him *and* Alfred whenever my parents needed them to, my parents formally adopted Ossie. They did this over the phone and neither my parents nor Ossie ever saw the market stall holder ever again.

Within a very short time Ossie became very close to my mum. As close as Alfred to my dad. He really didn't like it when she wasn't around to cuddle him and he *loooooved* all the *mimos* he was given on a daily basis. Once, when he was staying over at Auntie Dee's and Uncle Vini's, he famously ate a large chunk of Auntie Dee's favourite sweatshirt and the corner of her duvet cover just to make sure he didn't have to stay with them forever.

Ossie also didn't particularly like sleeping downstairs in his own bed next to Alfred's, but he didn't have a choice because by now my parents had installed a baby gate at the top of the stairs, to give Neffie some peace and quiet upstairs.

So every night when my parents went to bed, Ossie would come up the stairs and lie down on the last step right in front the the baby gate. My mum would then get up again, pick him up, kiss him and carry him downstairs to his own bed. There he and Alfred would both receive a goodnight doggie biscuit, and that was the end of their daily routine. They kept it up until the day Ossie died, and during the three years he lived with my parents Ossie finally felt safe and happy. And I guess you could say that he also healed my mum's broken heart.

Ossie and Alfred were never particularly close, but they made do. They even shared a bed on the odd occasion, although most of the time Ossie stole Alfred's much bigger bed and Alfred... um... let him... And then was forced to sleep in Ossie's much smaller bed, with his bottom and head hanging out over the sides.

And all the while nobody knew that they would only have three short years together. Because unbeknownst to them Ossie wasn't just crooked and lop-sided with a set of mightily rotten teeth, but inside himself he had a big, bad cancer that silently grew and grew whilst Ossie was finally having the time of his life.

And that's the thing with life, you just never know how much time you have left. Which is why people say that you have to try to enjoy every day as if it was your last. Of course most people don't really do it, even though they say it.

For three years Ossie was happy and fine until suddenly from one day to the next he wasn't fine anymore. Nobody knew anything was wrong with him though until the day he peed blood. And then he started panting and wouldn't stop panting anymore. Then everyone freaked out. Especially my mum and dad. And then they took him to the vet who told them to go see a specialist.

On the day they finally got an appointment with the specialist my dad couldn't be with my mum and Ossie because he was meant to be working out of town. Since he needed the car to do so, he dropped my mum off at the specialist vet's surgery on the way, which happened to be in the middle of nowhere, somewhere in the Essex countryside outside East London. The plan was to get some scans done and then for my mum and Ossie to return home by bus.

But of course that's not what happened. Ossie had his scans alright, while my mum was pacing up and down some country lane like a mad woman, praying that he would be alright after all. When she returned to the surgery at the appointed time, the vet's face gave it all away really. My mum's heart dropped right out of her body when the vet told her that poor Ossie's kidneys were riddled with cancer and that nothing could be done anymore. She cradled Ossie in her arms and he tried to crawl under her jumper because he always loved to do that when he felt low and wanted to feel as close as possible to her. And my mum stumbled outside, sat down on the verge with him and cried like there was no tomorrow. And there really wasn't.

Another woman who had come to see the vet with her own dog happened to see my mum crying with Ossie by the roadside and it made her cry too out of sympathy. And then she bundled my mum and Ossie into her car and drove them home. All the way back to East London. A complete stranger who happened to have a big heart. My mum never forgot her. She also never forgot the roundabout close to their home, because by the time they got there she started to cry in earnest again. And from that day onward she would always remember that horrible day whenever she came across the roundabout. She really came to loathe that roundabout a lot.

And Ossie must have known that things were coming to an end, but he hung on in there and waited for my dad to come home. It was late at night when my dad came back and Ossie was so pleased to see him. So my dad also sat down on the sofa and cuddled Ossie and talked to him. And then my parents discussed that they would take Ossie to their own vet the next morning to find out if maybe something could be done after all.

They tried putting Ossie in his bed, but this time, he got up immediately and stood on his shaky little legs, panting like mad and looked at them with his big brown pleading eyes. And luckily my parents understood. They would have never forgiven themselves if they hadn't.

My mum picked him up and held him tight and

then she walked with him and my dad into the kitchen. My mum was crying badly by now, but my dad told her she needed to be calm for Ossie, so he wouldn't be upset for her.

So she tried her very best to do just that. She held and stroked Ossie, and my dad held and stroked them both. And then my dad told Ossie that it was ok and just to let go.

My mum had always told my dad that FOR ONCE in their lives she didn't want to have to make the decision to put an animal to sleep, and with Ossie she finally got her wish. Because when my dad told him 'It's okay Ossie, just let go', Ossie did exactly that.

It was a Wednesday (yes, I know, *another* Wednesday), and Ossie took one last breath and died in my mum's arms. And although it was horrendous for my parents, it was the nicest thing for Ossie. He didn't have to go to the vet anymore, he didn't need any operations and any more needles and prodding and being scared. He died in the arms of the people he loved the most, who during three short years had given him hope and made him forget that there were bad people in the world who hurt little dogs.

And I know that that's the truth because he told me so.

Chapter 10

AUNTS AND UNCLES

Now, that I've told you all there is to know about my furry siblings, I bet you are curious to find out what happened to my human family after I last told you about them.

Well, Auntie Dee and Uncle Vini are still the same, although my uncle doesn't work at the shop anymore. They still meet up with my parents a lot, and then they remember the times when I was still around and we all used to hang out together. Of course they couldn't do it during the long time *Pan Demic* was in charge and didn't let them do this any longer. But they chatted a lot on the phone.

My aunt and uncle now sometimes look after the dogs of a friend, and at first I didn't like it at all. NOT ONE SINGLE BIT! Especially when they were allowed to use my food and drinking bowls – the ones my mum had given Auntie Dee and Uncle Vini for when I used to stay with them.

But then more time passed and I was busy doing other things over here, and I figured it was okay after all, and so I let them.

Uncle Richard and Auntie Marina missed me an awful lot, and all our many routines. And when they finally got to read my story, the one my mum helped me write, they cried a lot because they remembered it all so well.

Auntie Marina kept all my things at her house inside her secretaire – all the toys she bought me and all the treats I hadn't gotten around to eat before I died. All my pictures, too. Only my daybed got put in storage, because nobody needed any more reminders of what had happened.

And to this day, my toys and treats are still at Auntie Marina's. They all reckon that if I manage to come back as someone else, and I then were to march straight up to the secretaire demanding my ball and treats, it would be the easiest way to prove that it was really me.

Watch this space is all I can say!

From time to time my mum checks that all my things are still there. And then she kisses my green ball and looks at my pictures on the wall as she does so.

Did I tell you that Auntie Marina once saw me as a ghost? She did!

It was a month or so after I had died. On the day in question she was home alone and had started to feel unwell and feverish, but no one was there to notice because they had all gone to a funeral. And that's when she suddenly saw me in her study.

She told my mum afterwards, that I had felt very cold to touch and that she had tried to wrap her arms around me to warm me up.

But unfortunately she couldn't do that and so poor Auntie Marina ended up with a bad fever and pneumonia instead.

Luckily for her Uncle Richard had a hunch that something wasn't right and when my auntie didn't answer her phone when he tried ringing her after the funeral, he quickly ran back to her home and turned up just in time to save her life. She ended up in hospital that day and I stayed with her just to make sure she was okay. Luckily, after a few days she felt much better and was allowed go back home again.

She told my mum that she still feels me around her all the time. But she never saw me again.

And then soon afterwards *Pan Demic* started to get up to no good, and both my parents and Uncle Richard began to worry a lot about Auntie Marina, and her being alone in her house. So they all decided it would be best if she were to move in with Uncle Richard for the time being, until things got back to normal again. The original plan was for her to stay for three months, but you all know what happens to best-laid plans.

Three months turned into four, then five, then six, and before you know it almost two whole years had passed and she was still living with my uncle.

During all that time my parents took care of her house, my mum took care of my aunt and uncle's shopping, and Uncle Richard took care of Auntie Marina. They still are, and I reckon she will stay with my uncle now, as she feels safe there, and she loves being looked after by him. That way she's not lonely anymore, and she always has someone to talk to.

And as for our Sunday tea, coffee and cake routine, the one we always had at Auntie Marina's house, well that was moved to Uncle Richard's house once *Pan Demic* allowed it, and although I can't be there in person anymore, I still pop in from time to time whenever they all meet up. Unfortunately I can't clean myself on Uncle Richard's bathroom towels anymore, but then again, I don't need to either.

My Auntie Pachy who lives in Argentina is fine too. Because of *Pan Demic* my parents didn't get to see her again for a very long time, because nobody was allowed to travel. But they talked to her a lot on the phone.

Pushu, her cat, died during that time which really broke Auntie Pachy's heart. And when Pushu finally arrived over here, she blatantly ignored what my dad had told her when he last saw her alive. You might remember that he had asked her to 'say hello' to me when she died? Well, she didn't. Not 'hello' and not anything else either. Cats, I tell you!

I only briefly saw her once from a distance. I reckon she had better things to do. And frankly, so did I.

My aunties Barbara and Margaret are also well. Auntie Barbara didn't see or feel me again after the incident with the rubbish, where I had told her off for picking it up when my parents weren't home, by way of pushing against her leg with all my might. Remember? And like I told you, she only heard me bark the once shortly after I had died. She did feel me a few times in their house though, right next to the kitchen table, but soon afterwards I decided to move on and to leave her and Auntie Margaret in peace for good.

Chapter 11

GHOSTS AND DREAMS

Do you remember that I once told you that I used to be scared of ghosts? Well, I was. And I don't scare easily, as you know. I always thought they were very eerie, and it completely freaked me out that my parents for some strange reason couldn't see them. Sometimes walked right through them and didn't react in the slightest. Creepy!

Wasn't only at home though where I saw ghosts. No, they are literally everywhere. Mostly inside houses, popping in to see what's going on in their old homes. Uncle Richard's house has a few. One of them is a lady who smells like flowers when she visits, usually in the very early hours of the morning. My uncle can't see her, but he can smell her and he rather likes it when she comes around because he says she is a friendly ghost. He also talks to her but so far she's never answered back.

Auntie Marina's house also has a ghost, but that one only appears in one spot, usually once a month around the time of a full moon. Never understood why and so I stared at it a lot.

Oh, and then there was the house of my parents' friends. Their ghost I didn't like at all. He hogs the cupboard that is built into the wall right above the first few steps of their staircase and HATES when people touch it or come anywhere near it. Then he opens or shuts the cupboard door and throws things around in a temper when no one's watching, and leaves towels and stuff on the floor for people to find.

My mum reckons it's because he must have hidden something in the cupboard when was still alive and now he's terribly irate because he can't get to it anymore and wants to scare people off so they can't find it.

He thinks the house is still his and it makes him very cross that people dare to come and go as they please.

I thought he was really scary when I first saw him and made sure I stayed well away from him when my parents took me over to their friends' house for a visit one time. Everybody noticed how I felt about him too, which is why my mum always wanted to take me back there to check if I could still see him. But she never got around to doing so and I'm mightily glad she didn't.

Of course, all dogs can see ghosts, but some of us just ignore them. Not sure how anyone could possibly do that, but there you go.

Now of course I am not scared anymore because, well, for one you could say that I'm one of them now, but also because I now know that most of the ghosts are just people and animals that have ended up over here and sometimes can be seen on the other side. Or heard. Or smelled, for that matter. Some of them roam around and want to be seen, but others are either lost or kind of stuck where they are and don't know how to move on.

But I wanted to tell you about one ghost in particular. The one that visits our house from time to time and used to frighten me a lot because I could see him even though almost no one else could. He isn't always there, but comes and goes and when he does, he literally pops in suddenly like… well, like a ghost. One minute he's there, and the next minute he's gone. Poof! Just like that. But only on certain days and at certain times, mostly in the evening or at night.

Not exactly sure why, but my mum reckons it's something to do with anniversaries of important stuff that happened to him when he was still alive, and I think she might be right.

But let me go back a few years to when I was still around.

The story of the ghost begins with *Signor Gassi*.

Many years ago, right after Ossie had died, my parents bought a poster of a painting of a little dog and framed it. The dog in the picture looked nothing like Ossie, but there was just something about it that reminded my mum and dad of him. And then my mum started calling the little dog *Signor Gassi*. Not even going to *try* to explain why!

Anyway, by the time I arrived on the scene, the picture of *Signor Gassi* was hanging on the wall halfway up the last of our many staircases, the one right at the top of the house that leads to our bedroom. I'll let my mum tell you what happened next:

When we were just about to adopt Nelson, one of the things we were worried about was whether he would be able to climb the many stairs in our house with his rather short legs. The reason for our worries was that previously Alfred, who was a Scottish Terrier, had had real

120

difficulties doing so, possibly due to the fact that the stairs were almost black in colour and he therefore couldn't see them, and also because they were probably too slippery for his short Scottie legs.

And of course additionally because Alfred had a big problem with breaking rules once they had been established. In our London house the rule had been 'Don't go upstairs!' But whereas everyone else in the furry family blissfully ignored this rule, Alfred took it as written in stone and never once attempted to climb the staircase after he had once been told not to.

Then, when we moved house, he simply applied the same rule to his new home and found it almost impossible to get past it, even when we told him that we wanted him to go upstairs. We spent quite some time trying to coax him up the stairs to the living room, and even when we managed to finally persuade him that it was okay to climb the stairs after all, he would always have that spooked and almost pained look on his face of someone who has been caught in the act of doing something forbidden.

In the end Alfred climbed the stairs only extremely reluctantly, and only when accompanied by either one of us, and even then only to the first floor where the living room is, because he knew it was the only room that contained a rug, and he rather preferred a cosy rug to the exposed wooden floors in the rest of the house. He ignored all the other staircases completely and never once used them no matter how hard we tried to persuade him to do so.

But each time Alfred went up and down the stairs to

the living room he looked very much like someone who had put on ice skates for the very first time. He would wobble about, hesitate, slip and slide, and only be happy (and exhale audibly) when he was safely downstairs once more.

After Alfred's death, and shortly before we met Nelson for the first time, I read somewhere that dogs with short legs aren't really suited to houses with a lot of stairs, which is why we asked the people at the rescue centre where Nelson was staying at the time, if they thought climbing stairs would be a problem for him.

They told us that no, it wouldn't be a problem, but I have to admit that they looked at us as if we were slightly deranged for asking the question in the first place. And we only understood why when we brought Nelson home that day. Because instead of testing out each step gingerly and then taking ages to get up to the next floor like Alfred had done, Nelson simply raced up right to the top at once, and almost seemed to be oblivious to the fact that there was a staircase there in the first place. It was very much a case of he wanted to go upstairs and he was going to go upstairs, never mind the obstacle.

He did the same on the way down, and at breakneck speed too, never once stopping to see if each shiny dark brown step would hold his weight like Alfred had done in the past.

And this is precisely why, after some time had passed, we noticed immediately when Nelson, all of a sudden, wouldn't go past the picture of Signor Gassi anymore.

He was completely fine on all the other staircases, but on this one he would come to a sudden halt right next to the picture, as if he had hit an invisible wall, and then he would start to whine and not go any further. Even stranger still, he would try to get past it, but each time we observed him do so, it looked as if he was straining against an invisible barrier he simply couldn't cross.

But it gets even more bizarre. If either of us then told him 'Come on up!' or 'It's okay, Nellie' or something of the sort, he would simply race past the picture no problem at all. We couldn't figure it out. This went on for weeks until we finally accepted that this was going to be the way it was from now on.

Then one day we had a couple of guests to stay, one of whom told us an amazing story about our house.

Apparently, many years ago, when he was still a young man, our guest befriended a builder, called Mr J, who was in the process of renovating what was then not yet our house. And as Mr J was working his way all the way from the top of the house right down to the bottom, repairing everything that needed repairing as he went along, one afternoon he suddenly spotted a man on one of the staircases in what he thought was fancy dress, who was making his way slowly down the stairs. He later said that the man had been dressed like a cavalier from the 17th century. Mr J was very surprised to find someone inside the house and therefore called out to the man. But the man didn't react at all and just kept on walking. And only when he disappeared into thin air before his very eyes, did Mr J realise that he had seen a ghost.

He was completely spooked by the experience and quickly ran outside and down the road to the garage nearby where his friend worked. Mr J then told his friend what had happened and begged him to come with him immediately and to also bring his dog along, because he wanted to see if the dog would pick up something unusual about the house. But by the time they all got back to the house, the cavalier had long gone and not even the dog could get a whiff of him any longer.

Unsurprisingly, Mr J wasn't really keen to work alone in the house after that, but after a few days he reluctantly decided to return as the renovation work needed to be completed.

Luckily for him, he never saw the cavalier again, but when he had finally worked his way all the way down to the basement, he found a metal statue of a cavalier there, and nobody knew where it had come from.

After his experience, Mr J decided it was only fitting to put the statue up on a plinth outside the house, halfway up the wall. And that is where it resides to this very day.

Here's another spooky fact for you: when my mum asked the guest who had told her about Mr J and the ghost to show her exactly where in our house the cavalier had appeared and disappeared, guess where that happened to be! Oh yes, halfway up the top staircase, PRECISELY next to the picture of *Signor Gassi*!

Of course it was! That's why I didn't want to go past him!

But not long after my parents found out about the ghost, I decided to try my hardest to ignore him. Well, okay, I DID stare at the staircase quite a bit whenever the cavalier put in an appearance, but I found a way of avoiding the staircase whenever he was around.

My mum and dad never saw the ghost of the cavalier by the way, but then they don't see me now either, which is highly annoying.

But their niece saw him and it completely freaked her out, too.

She was sleeping on my sofa in the living room at the time. That's just where the staircase the ghost uses, ends. She slept quite peacefully until the early hours of the morning, when she suddenly woke up and saw someone standing in the middle of the room looking at her. But because she was still very sleepy and had her eyes only half open, she only glimpsed that it was a man with longish hair and therefore immediately assumed it was my dad who must have forgotten something in the living room and had come down to get it.

Of course, come the next morning, my dad told her that he hadn't. And that's when his niece suddenly remembered after all that the man she had seen *had* worn a brimmed hat and rather strange clothes…

Needless to say, she didn't sleep that well the following night. But luckily for her, the cavalier didn't put in another appearance during the rest of her stay.

In the first days after I had died, and because my parents couldn't see me, my mum was hoping very much that I would at least be able to send her a sign from the Other Side, like DeNiro – and Ossie after him – had done. But sometimes when you want things too badly they just don't happen. Don't ask me why, but I think it's something to do with energy.

And that's why, even though I barked 'Mummy, I'm right here!' as loudly as I could over here, she didn't hear me over there. And so she didn't get the sign she so desperately wanted.

But instead she got to meet me in a dream.

And yes, of course it's possible to meet up in dreams! It's just that people usually don't believe that it has really happened, and when they wake up afterwards they doubt what they've seen. Of course not all dreams are true either.

My mum always used to say that some dreams are just dreams, but others are somehow *more*. And those ones are amazing, because you get to travel and really see things. Some people even end up over here on the Other Side, even though they're not dead. They're just lost in one of those dreams that are *more*, and they don't realise where they are, and usually someone over here has to send them back home.

Anyway, my mum was never completely sure if it had been one of *those* dreams when she met me, but she sure hopes it was.

I'll let her tell you in her own words – it's her dream after all:

It was the strangest thing. I remember being aware that I was in a dream as soon as I saw Nelson standing in front of me. And I was intensely grateful that I was getting another chance to say goodbye. Nelson didn't really move. He just stood there and let me hug and kiss him. His

127

Auntie Dee was there too, standing right behind me, which is why I had to turn around and away from Nelson to look at her. And every time I did this, I was anxiously wondering if Nelson would still be there when I turned towards him once more, because deep down I knew that any moment now he would have to go away. He stayed for a while longer, and I was grateful for every second he did, but of course the last time I turned towards him he had gone.

And no, I'm not allowed to tell you if it really happened. Rules are rules over here, too. And I know a thing or two about rules, if you remember.

Chapter 12

MEMORIES

My mum once read somewhere that when you yawn at a dog and they're on the same wavelength as you, they will yawn back. They call it an *empathy* yawn – whatever that is.

So, my mum being my mum, decided to try this theory out on me on the very day my parents first brought me home after they had adopted me. And my dad took photos while she yawned at me. My parents are still laughing about it now, because OF COURSE I yawned right back at her. In fact, seeing her yawn made me yawn so badly that in the photos my dad took my mouth is so wide open that I almost look like a shark. Which made my mum call me *Tiburón* for a while... Well, she would, wouldn't she!

While I was busy doing my rounds over here, getting to know the place, I kept remembering things like that from my old life. *Sooooo* many memories, funny and sad. The sad ones I don't really want to keep.

Like the time when I got ill and the vet took one of my legs off. I really had a go at him about it when I woke up afterwards, and made damn sure neither he nor any of the nurses could touch me ever again. Not even when I was still completely groggy and half asleep from my ordeal and in serious need of tons of *mimos* and reassurance.

And to add insult to injury, the vet then called me a weird name when I raced over to my parents on my three remaining legs and straight into their waiting arms, as soon as the nurses let me out of the horrible cage they had kept me in. As my mum and dad were stroking and kissing me to make me feel better, I heard the vet say, 'This one's a right little *Jackal and Hide*!'. Not *exactly* sure what he meant by that. Well, ok, the 'Jackal' bit I got – probably snarled like one when he dared touch me as I came around from being under. But what's with the 'Hide'??? Never hid my dislike for him for one single second, I can tell you!

No, the bad memories I definitely don't want to keep! But the funny and the happy ones are great fun to remember.

Like the time my Uncle Vini and Auntie Dee stayed over for the night one time. Because our house isn't that big, and the guest room was already being used, they had to sleep on the living room floor on a mattress, which was great because it meant that I had super easy access to Uncle Vini's head and could lick his face and head to my heart's content anytime I chose to do so. Mostly in the middle of the night. Or *very* early in the morning when he was too sleepy to defend himself. He always got double the attention, too because Auntie Dee doesn't like her face to be licked at all, which is why I made sure that Uncle Vini got her share of all the *mimos* on top of his own.

In the morning everyone would take turns to have their shower in the upstairs bathroom. Now, I should explain that there are three hooks at the back of the door in our bathroom that my parents use to hang up their towels. And then, just slightly to the right of them, is another, separate hook where my own towel used to hang. Well away from theirs because it always used to be covered from top to bottom in my white hair. Remember? I told you I was shedding tons of the stuff on a daily basis.

Anyway, that morning in question, when Uncle Vini finally got up to have a shower, he must have been quite tired still, *possibly* due to the fact that he had woken up numerous times during the night thanks to my constant licking of his head. We will never know.

I think his eyes must not have been fully open when he finally opened the shower door to get out. And that's possibly why, as he was grappling blindly for his towel, his hand must have strayed *ever so slightly* to the right…

Next thing we heard him shout 'WHICH TOWEL DID YOU SAY AGAIN WAS MINE?' That's because, after having dried himself thoroughly with the towel he had gotten hold of, he must have caught sight of himself in the bathroom mirror and seen the state he was in. Let me put it this way: I had never seen my uncle white and hairy like me before. Basically, he went into the shower looking like himself and came out looking like a Yeti! Needless to say, he had to shower all over again. And this time he made damn sure not to use my towel again.

Something else I remembered was what my dad refers to as 'the rabbit incident'.

It took place on a beautiful late summer's day. We were all out on a walk and I was having a great time racing around on the East Hill in the Country Park just behind our house. My mum and dad were walking along the cliffs on the far side and I was running about, sniffing this, sniffing that, peeing here, peeing there – as you do.

Suddenly I spotted a rabbit in the distance and decided I'd better make sure he wasn't up to any mischief on *my* hill. So I raced over to him and quickly scooped him up with my mouth. I hadn't quite decided yet whether to take him home or what to do with him, but that's when my mum spotted us and began to howl like a banshee.

You see, my mum loves all animals and I guess she wasn't too pleased at the sight of a rabbit dangling out of my mouth. She screeched so loudly, I immediately dropped the rabbit just to shut her up. The rabbit was shaken, but otherwise fine and completely unharmed, and he quickly did a hasty runner and hopped face first into the first rabbit hole he could find, just in case I happened to change my mind about taking him home.

Luckily for my ears, my mum, seeing the rabbit escape unhurt, stopped her screaming. But then she started to wail 'THANK *YOUUUU*!'. And then she just kept repeating it over and over and over again. To tell you the truth I had never heard her say 'Thank you!' so many times in a row. In fact, she said it so many times that I was beginning to wonder if she would ever say anything else ever again. My dad and I were mightily relieved when

133

she finally stopped, I can tell you! And I never put another rabbit in my mouth ever again.

Another thing I remembered also took place up on the East Hill. Must have been one of the first times my mum ever took me there. It was a windy day and we were walking along, just her and I, when all of a sudden the heavens opened and it started to hail. I remember my mum was wearing a long woollen cardigan at the time, but no raincoat. And I wasn't wearing anything. At first it only rained with sleety bits mixed in, but soon it started to hail in earnest. And I mean BIG chunky bits of ice! They were pelting down on us relentlessly and hit us all over and really hurt my nose and head.

All over the hill people were running for cover, but my mum realised we were never going to make it to safety, and so instead of running, she dropped down on her knees in the wet grass and opened her woollen cardigan wide so I could creep inside. But because I am very long and my bottom was sticking out, she had to arch over me like a human tent so no part of me would get hurt by the hailstones.

We huddled together like that for what seemed like ages with the hail relentlessly pummelling my mum's back. And all the while she was holding me tight and stroking me, and kissing and nibbling my ears, and telling me it would all be okay.

I remember it well, just her and I on top of the hill, and how she smelled that day, and how safe and warm I felt. And how when we finally got up, my mum's cardigan had expanded so much thanks to the soaking it had received, that it now reached the floor and almost tripped her up. It never went back to its original size either, but my mum just didn't care. She had a good laugh about it, and so did my dad when we both finally got back home looking like two bedraggled poodles.

My parents also remember tons of things about our life together. The other day I overheard my dad reminding my mum of something else that made him laugh a lot when he remembered it.

You see, one thing my dad says he really loved about me, was the fact that I was ambitious. For example when it came to sticks, no stick was ever big or long enough for me, so technically they were actually more branches than sticks, and most of them were around five times my size. At least!

Yes, the bigger the better was definitely my

motto. And never mind that I could barely carry them. But believe me, even though the muscles on my neck were bulging like crazy, carry them I did.

I had the same attitude when it came to pebbles and stones, but with those I had little choice in the matter, because I had to make do with whatever my parents picked up and threw for me.

Now, on the day I was going to tell you about, a happy afternoon spent finding pebbles my dad had thrown for me (because my mum can't throw to save her life!) was coming to an end. But since I had such fun with my last pebble and didn't want to leave it behind where another dog could find and possibly nick it, I decided to take it back home with me. But I knew from past experience that in my parents' book this was a complete and utter 'NO-NO'. The reason for this being that I had already once successfully managed to sneak another pebble back home with me by hiding it inside my mouth, right at the back of my throat.

Now, you may remember that I had always had *slight* issues with letting go when I was still your side of things. As in 'Once something is mine, IT STAYS MINE!'. Which is why I then had the nightmare task of guarding the pebble I had brought home with me. Which in turn turned into a right nightmare for my parents, too, as they weren't allowed to come anywhere near it. And yes, that included sitting on their own sofa.

I would growl as soon as anyone came near the

pebble to make sure they got the drift and would become so obsessed with the whole guarding-it-thing, that I couldn't even let it out of my sight for a single second. Not even to eat my dinner. The whole thing became quite unpleasant and stressful for everyone involved. Myself included.

And that's why my parents decided never to let me take another pebble home again. EVER! No sticks either, by the way.

So, I knew that day on the beach that I had to hide the last pebble well if I wanted to be able to bring it back home with me.

I tried hiding it inside my mouth as best as I could, but unfortunately for me the pebble turned out to be quite a bit of a gobstopper. I couldn't even close my teeth around it. Never mind my mouth. So I put my head down and started to briskly walk back home, making sure that I was always in front of my parents, so they wouldn't see what I was carrying half in, half out of my mouth.

So then we get to the front door, and that's when my dad realises I've got a gob full of pebble. And he tells me firmly – and completely in vain – to 'LEAVE IT!'

Only… I just wouldn't. No way! Not EVER!

So I just stood there on the doorstep, gritting my teeth against the pebble in mute protest.

Next thing my dad tries to wrench the pebble out of my gaping mouth, but I've got very strong yaws, and short of ripping my teeth out, he can't do much to dislodge the pebble.

Now my mum is also telling me to 'LEAVE IT!' but of course by now we've gone past the point of no return as far as either of us is concerned, and NO WAY, WOULD I EVER let them win now! Nuh-uh – not in a million years!!

And of course deep down my parents know this.

Also, by now I simply cannot back down, because that would mean losing face and not just my pebble. And neither can my dad. For the same reason. Minus the pebble. So it's stand-off time.

But then my dad has the bright idea of closing the front door in my face, so I have to stand outside, still on the lead, pebble firmly in mouth, and my parents stand inside, lead in hand, listening and waiting by the door until such time when I finally deign to drop the pebble.

I guess you could say I stood there for quite some time, drool pooling at my feet, because that's what happens when you can't close your mouth properly.

From time to time my parents would open the door to check on the state of affairs, and I would stare right back at them, teeth still firmly clamped around my pebble. Then the door would close again, and we all waited to see who would give up first.

When the pebble got too heavy at long last, I put it down at my feet, only to quickly snatch it up again when the door was opened the next time. Did that quite a few times, come to think of it.

Time went by and my parents were starting to wonder what the neighbours were thinking about what was going on.

In the end they bribed me with a treat. Believe me, I ignored it as long as I possibly could, but the treat just smelled *soooo gooood*, which was torture and also made the drooling worse.

Also, by now it was nearly dinnertime and I *was* rather tired of standing outside my own front door.

So, finally and against all my convictions, I pointedly put the pebble down for the last time, my mum quickly shortened my lead so I couldn't change my mind again, and my traitorous dad sent my beloved pebble flying down the road with a well-aimed kick, just as I was about to take the treat they were offering me.

NOT. NICE. AT. ALL!!!

I guess that was one of the few times in my life where I had to (ungraciously) admit defeat. Then again, I *did* get an extra treat, and at least I didn't have to stay awake all night long to guard the pebble.

But after that palaver I never brought another pebble home with me.

Too much hassle by far.

Chapter 13

FINAL GOODBYE?

Some people look for white feathers as a sign from the departed, but for my parents it's white hair. *My* white hair.

It still turns up in the most surprising places even though *soooo* much time has passed since I went away. And no, it's not because my parents don't clean the house. They do. All the time. Which is why, my dad says, it's extra special when it happens, because he says it's almost impossible after all this time. And every time it does, my parents smile a lot because it makes them happy to think that little bits of me still linger on.

I just popped over one last time to see if anything has changed back home. It's Christmas again and Heloir is standing underneath the Christmas tree once more. Billy got to hang out with my parents again this year, and I *almost* didn't mind. Heloir doesn't mind either as there really is no danger of him getting nipped by anyone anymore.

Raúl, our car, is still around too, but he's getting really old now, and my mum is dreading the day when he won't be around any longer. Because he knew and carried all of us; every single member of my family. And of course he's the one who carried me to my forever home on my very first journey with my parents.

And away from it on my very last…

My house looks pretty much the same as it did when I was still around. My parents still miss me a lot, but it's not so raw anymore, and they trust that if it's meant to be, I'll find my way back home again. And on the days my mum finds it hard to deal with the fact that she doesn't feel me around any longer, she picks up Hugo, one of my favourite toys, and she puts him to her nose and inhales deeply. Because she never washed him after I died and he still smells of me. Just faintly, but the smell is *just about* still there. And she makes sure she doesn't hold him for too long so he doesn't lose it.

And then my mum remembers how I used to shake Hugo and rip him open YET AGAIN, and that she had to sew him up once more for the umpteenth time. But of course, first she had to wrestle him from my snarling mouth.

And sometimes Mummy still whispers 'Nellie, where are you?' when she thinks nobody is listening. And occasionally she still cries in the car when they play a song on the radio that reminds her of me.

And from time to time she still takes Clara, my other favourite toy, with her when my parents go away on holiday. Clara then gets to sleep in the dip between my parents where I used to lie.

Papá is composing a lot as always, and now and then I still pop up in his music, and my mum is spending a lot of time writing my story. And it feels as if the time is almost right for me to try to find my way back home for good.

143

They tell me when you come back you won't remember a thing, but I reckon we'll see about that!

Maybe it just depends on how strongly you fix your memories in your mind and heart. And so I make sure to do just that.

I take one last look back at everything, taking it all in, every single, little thing: my house, my street, my family.

The way you can easily spot everything that is going on down below in my street from the comfort of my sofa through my window.

The way the sun glitters on the sea in the distance when it's nice outside, and the rain pelts the windowpanes when it's not.

The way the wind shakes our house and makes the windows rattle during a storm. And I remember chasing the foam on the pebbles on the beach whenever the sea was angry and rough.

The way the grass tickles my back when I stick up all my paws in the air and try to scratch my back on the ground by wriggling around like mad. And I remember the warmth of the sun on my belly and all the nice smells in the air as I roll about and suddenly tumble all the way down the hill, which makes my parents howl with laughter.

The way the water in the muddy pool of my favourite creek always feels so cool on my tummy as I jump right in on one of my many walks. And I remember sticking my head right in, searching for sticks and whatever else lies beneath, only to come up coughing and spluttering, having learned the hard way that trying to breathe under water isn't exactly the brightest idea.

The way my dad sits on the sofa while he's composing. He's bent over slightly and his fingers are moving very fast over the keys of the thin metal box on his lap. And now and then he stops and glances down to his right where I used to lie, pressed up tightly against his leg. And I remember how it used to feel to be so close to him, and how I would quickly lick his fingers whenever they came to rest anywhere near my head before he could object. Because he says you can't compose with sticky fingers.

The way my mum sometimes dances in our living room early in the morning. Her arms are swirling through the air and every now and then she blows a kiss to the painting my Uncle Vini made of me. And I remember how it used to feel when she was kissing the sides of my face next to my mouth between each move, and how I managed to get a lick in now and then which made her laugh and squeal '*Nooooo, Nelliebelly!* No licking!' because she was a bit grossed out imagining where my tongue had been just seconds before.

The way my Uncle Vini sneaks me some food in the kitchen or off the table, before anyone can object. And I remember what his head and face taste like each time I thoroughly clean them with my tongue.

The way Auntie Dee strokes my head as I lounge around lazily in the sun on my sofa. And I remember how she, and my aunties Barbara and Margaret, always made sure I had my very own sofa replacement pushed right up to the window of their own houses whenever I got to stay over so I wouldn't miss the view from my own.

The way Uncle Richard kisses my growling nose whenever we play pull with my ball and feels completely safe doing so, even though my teeth are only inches away from his face. But he and I both know that if his hands were to stray even the tiniest bit towards my back or my bottom all bets would be off.

The way my mum immediately sits up straight on the sofa whenever I touch her leg with my paw to let her know that it's time to let me climb onto her lap. But I have to sit up straight so I won't hang awkwardly over the edge of her knees because my body is just too long for her legs. And I remember how good it felt to have my back and scruff massaged for hours on end on her lap this way.

The way it feels to race towards my dad each time my mum asks me 'Where's Papá?' when we go outside to meet him and I suddenly spot him in the distance waving his arms at me. And I remember how proud I felt when he ruffled my fur and stroked me and told me 'Well done! You found me!' when I finally caught up with him.

The way it feels to fling myself off the cliff path into my mum's waiting arms as she stands on the rock below. And I remember that it took all the courage I possessed to do so, but I just knew that she would catch me every single time and that she would never let me fall.

The way my parents kiss each other goodnight and then say goodnight to me too, even though I'm not there any longer. And I remember how safe it felt to bury myself deeply into the duvet right in the space between them.

So many memories…

I fix them firmly in my heart and mind.

Now all I need to do is to REMEMBER.

Time to go now, I think.

I'll see you on the other side…

THE END?

MY PHOTO GALLERY

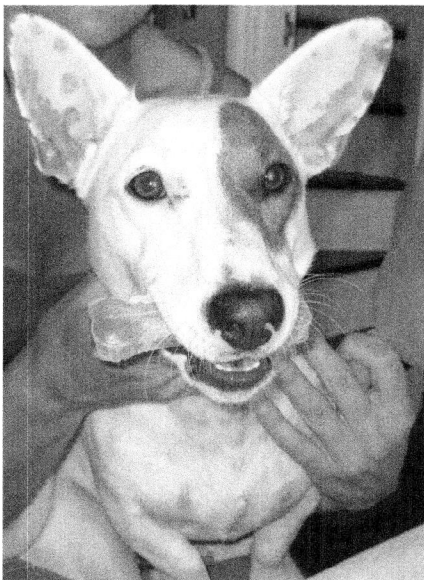

This is me, guarding my bone…

… *and* my window!

Waiting for my dad to stop working so we can go out and play

Finally! With my dad on the beach

Couldn't find a bigger stick, so this one had to do

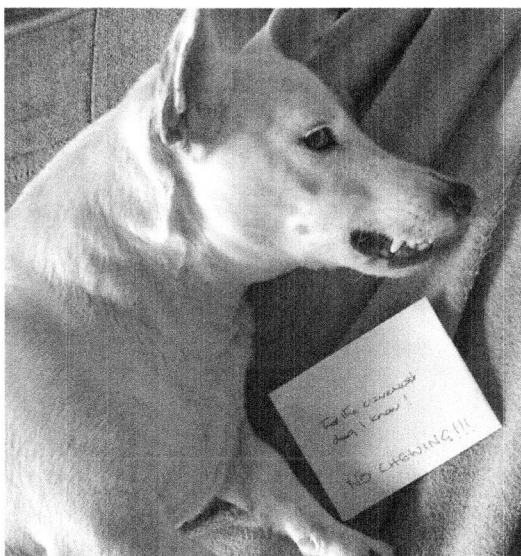

Never liked being told what to do. Not even by Auntie Marina...

Me objecting strongly to my dad's suggestion we go and visit
the creepy crypt…

… but of course they took me there anyway! And I didn't even
get to take away a souvenir!

Chilling with my mum…

Whose idea was that duvet cover?

Hanging out with Auntie Dee and Uncle Vini...

... and with Auntie Marina and Uncle Richard

Auntie Pachy quickly rubbing my belly before I can object…

My *empathy* yawn on the day I first met my mum - remember?!!
LOADS of empathy there, as you can see!

Early days. A tiny DeNiro with my mum

DeNiro seriously contemplating climbing up my mum's hair…

Comfy snooze in the afternoon

See if you can spot DeNiro…

Drawers are the best!

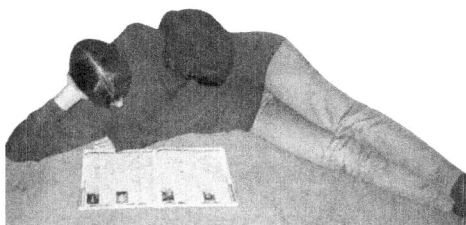
DeNiro reading with my mum

DeNiro in later life

DeNiro and Neffie on top of
my parents' bunk bed

Nefertiti aka Neffie

DeNiro and Neffie snoozing with my mum

A very happy Alfred with my dad

Alfred inching ever closer
to Heloir

Alfred waiting for the fox

Still waiting…

Alfred on his beloved rug

Ossie with my mum

Ossie having a whale of a time in my dad's hammock

Ossie and Alfred

Guess who's hogging the bed
AGAIN!

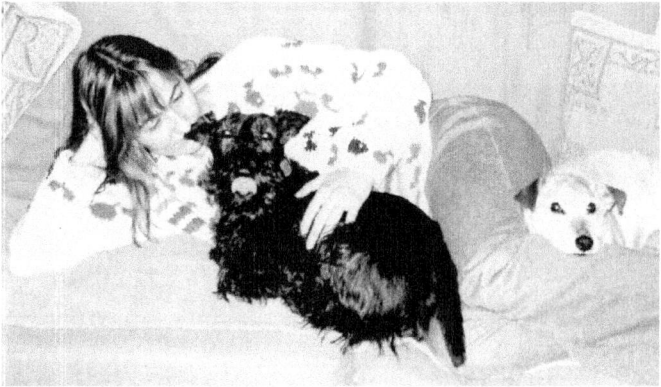

Too many cuddles by far for Alfred's liking...

Billy showing off his underbite

Billy doing his best frog impression

Billy hoping if he stares long and hard enough at the plate it
will miraculously come closer

"Miss" Gracie

Gracie refusing to walk

Billy freaking out because Gracie fixes him with her stare

I REALLY miss being in the back of Raúl, our car…

… and going away on holiday with my mum and dad

But this…

… and this I miss the most…

AUTHOR'S NOTE

After I finished writing Nelson's story back in 2020, I didn't really think that I would write another book. Yes, I know, I hinted at the end of the first book that Nelson was nudging me to write some more, but I honestly wasn't sure that I would actually do it. Nelson, of course, would now say 'Shouldn't have underestimated me then!'.

And so, as he kept insisting in that never-*EVER*-give-up way he and his dad share, I finally gave in and wrote this second book. The rest you know, because in it he told you what happened next.

The funny thing is that deep down I don't think that he's quite done yet either, but whether that will actually lead to a third book is very much up to him now.

Of course, if he really manages to come back home for good somehow, I'll definitely write about it, and if you sign up to my readers list, you'll be the first to know if or when that happens:

martinamars.com/contact

By signing up you will also get a **FREE** eBook copy of ***My Brother Alfred***, a short story about Nelson's brother Alfred, the Scottie dog, told once again in Nelson's inimitable style (of course!).

So, I guess for now this is very much an open ending and I am as curious as everyone else to find out what happens next.

And so far Nelson hasn't piped up to let me know what that will be…

Hastings, July 2022

ACKNOWLEDGMENTS

First and foremost, I would like to thank everyone who read – and continues to read – Nelson's story. I once said, by doing so you are keeping him alive, and I meant it!

Thanks to all of you who contacted me because you also lost someone you loved and therefore could relate to Nelson's story. Thank you for all your lovely emails, comments and reviews, and for telling me you fell in love with Nelson in spite, or possibly because, of his truculent ways – even though he probably wouldn't have reciprocated the sentiment in quite the same way had he still been around…

I would also like to thank Fiona Wilson, for once more being up for finding and erasing any mistakes I had made – any remaining mistakes are my own; my husband Polo Piatti and Nelson's Auntie Dee and Uncle Richard for reading my first draft and for not telling me to chuck it in the bin, as I had secretly feared they would do.

Thanks to Paul Knight for "polishing" all the photos once again, and for always being so ready to help out and having a chat about spooky matters – here's to ghosts and things that go bump in the night!

And I will always be grateful to Nelson for his final parting gift of this strange writing bug, and for continuing to nudge me to write some more.

ABOUT THE AUTHOR

Martina Mars is an actress and former dancer and as such has had all the usual – and unusual – daytime jobs in her time. She lives with her husband in East Sussex in the UK, and since Nelson doesn't stop nudging her to write some more, she is currently doing exactly that.

Also by Martina Mars:

I AM NELSON
The story of a little dog who is larger than life. Even when he's dead

My Brother Alfred
A little Scottie dog finds his forever home. A short story

Download your own **FREE** copy of
My Brother Alfred
here:
www.martinamars.com/free-ebook

FREE eBOOK OFFER

Get your own **FREE** copy of

My Brother Alfred
A little Scottie dog finds his forever home. A short story

here:

www.martinamars.com/free-ebook

Printed in Great Britain
by Amazon